AND THE DAWN CAME UP LIKE THUNDER . . . THE CIRCLE

Dedication

I dedicate this book and all that it stands for to the late Lady Mountbatten, to a lady who spent a great part of her life in the service of mankind. In many lands she was known for the genuine understanding she felt for all those who suffered or were in adversity. Her devotion to her great husband, Lord Mountbatten of Burma, and all he represented was an example of the finest quality to all people. To us P.O.W.'s just released by the victorious forces of her husband, she was something of an angel of mercy. Never at any time overconscious of her high rank, she swept into our filthy huts and hospital camps, bringing with her a clean purity and dynamic personality that lifted us out of the apathy that had befallen many of our numbers. Realising that to over sympathise with those who had forgotten that they were once men would be fatal, she brought them out of their mental coma with a vitality that was infectious to all who met her. To those of us who had waited, year after year, for the release that many had already given up hope for, Lord Louis was already a household word and when, finally, the great day arrived it was with immense emotion – I think felt by us all – that we saw both he and his wonderful wife drive into Changi Jail.

Though some feet away from both of them, I personally could feel the great magnetism they both possessed and in a matter of minutes the crowd of released prisoners were aware of it too. We felt we had known them all our lives. It was then I realised, though we as soldiers had not been fortunate enough to serve directly under his command, the great mental power Lord Mountbatten conveyed to all who met him – and Lady Mountbatten had that great power too.

We, who had been brainwashed by the Japanese in a thousand ways, had been reinstated as human beings again.

It is to her memory, and the fine things in life she stood and worked for, that this book is dedicated.

LEO RAWLINGS

Leo Rawlings

And The Dawn Came up Like Thunder . . . The Circle

And I beheld the dawn
   Coming up like thunder
Such as I had never
   seen before –
And I knew a great evil
   was to come –
That must be endured –
   and conquered –
Or I would die.

Burton Publishing & Communications

First published in Great Britain 1972
by Rawlings Chapman Publications

Second Impression: 1972

First Paperback edition in Great Britain 1975
by Futura Publications Ltd

First translated into Japanese 1980
by Nagase Takashi

First paperback edition in Japan 1984
by Shakai-Shisosha Co., Tokyo

Second Edition published in Great Britain as paperback
incorporating 'The Circle' by
Burton Publishing & Communications 1984

Printed in Great Britain by
Colonna Press Ltd.
Hemel Hempstead, Herts.

Cover design — Kay Jordan

ISBN 0 9508973 1 0

BUGLE BOOKS

Burton Publishing & Communications
PO Box 200, Watford. WD2 7LT

From thousands who walked, worked and survived –
In the valley of the shadow of death –
There was one who also walked, worked and survived
And recorded his thoughts, the agony he saw,
The heroism – the Unbelievable Truth –
In order that others might understand –
AND REMEMBER THOSE WHO DIED FOR THEM

FOREWORD

I know of no photographs or films which show the unbelievably ghastly life led by our unfortunate prisoners of war in the hands of the Japanese.

Fortunately one of our prisoners, Mr. Leo Rawlings, had the courage and the persistence, as well as the skill, to portray the horrifying life led by our prisoners of war.

He has written his story in this book. It is a story which must move everybody who admires the wonderful guts of our men while prisoners of the Japanese.

Mountbatten of Burma
A. F.

BRIGADIER THE LORD RUSSELL OF LIVERPOOL, C.B.E., M.C.

'Several of the paintings and drawings by Mr. Leo Rawlings in this Book depicting the conditions under which the prisoners employed on the Burma-Siam railway lived appeared as illustrations in my book of Japanese war crimes entitled 'THE KNIGHTS OF BUSHIDO'.

Early in 1942 IMPERIAL GENERAL HEADQUARTERS in Tokyo decided that a railway should be built across part of Siam and Burma for strategic purposes to shorten the line of communication between the Japanese armies in India and Burma and this was built by Allied prisoners of war who should not, under the terms of the Geneva Convention, have been employed on its construction.

The chief concern of the Japanese was that the railway should be completed in time to use it in resisting the Allied advance in Burma. The cost in lives and suffering mattered nothing. The prisoners of war could be driven like slaves, beaten, tortured and murdered by their Japanese and Korean guards so long as the target date was kept. They could die like flies of disease or malnutrition so long as the work went on.

Out of 46,000 Allied prisoners of war who were employed on this work, 16,000 died, and many thousands more will suffer from the effects of their ill-treatment for the rest of their lives.

The IMPERIAL GENERAL STAFF got its railway but at an appalling cost of human life and human suffering. Each mile of this 'Railroad of Death' was paid for with the lives of sixty-four Allied prisoners of war, and two hundred and forty coolie slaves.

Leo Rawlings was captured at the fall of Singapore, spending three and a half years as a prisoner of the Japanese, during which time he was put to work on the notorious railway. While a prisoner, he made over a hundred eye-witness paintings of the conditions under which the prisoners lived, producing them under the most difficult conditions with Chinese Indian ink, paints, crushed sandstone, clays and vegetable juices'.

Russell of Liverpool

The importance of this volume of one person's experiences in Japanese captivity lies in the pictorial record it presents. Very little was done or could be done to record for the future historian the appalling conditions experienced. Apparently no film and very little else in the way of photographic or graphic evidence survives, so that Mr. Rawlings' book stands in a unique category.

The pictures and sketches reveal the different styles he used, often changes imposed on him by the difficult nature of the materials he employed. A selection of his work now rests in the Imperial War Museum and photographs of all his wartime sketches and paintings have been added to the Museum's records.

Dr. C. H. Roads.
The Deputy Director
Imperial War Museum.

THE WELLCOME HISTORICAL MEDICAL MUSEUM AND LIBRARY

The Wellcome Building, Euston Road, London, N.W.1

Director:
F. N. L. Poynter, Ph.D. F.R.S.L., F.L.A.

'*The Wellcome Historical Medical Museum saw fit to purchase a number of paintings made by Leo Rawlings while a prisoner of war in Burma, to add to their existing collection of drawings of medical interest from various centres of war.*'

I think the publishing of this personal account of Leo Rawlings' P.O.W. paintings fills a gap in the story of the men who lived or died in the Far East prison camps, according to their strength or their refusal to give in under conditions which, even from the security of time, remain full of horror.

It was easy to believe when the war ended that never again would another be permitted. But the passage of time can bring false security and the mind can be dulled to the truth: this is why I think my old friend's book is a timely reminder to those of us who have still to learn the bitter lesson others were taught many years ago in Singapore.

These paintings are so horrifyingly correct, and tragically life-like, there is no need for words to support their message.

In the prison camps, life was communal. The 'loner' seldom lived long enough to contribute towards the day of liberation. And the paintings survived because of the help Leo received from many of his comrades.

Even if some find it possible now to forgive, this book may help everyone to realise that the sufferings in that land and the war that caused this must never be forgotten. The memory of the boys who died demands this of us all.

Bill Barclay Duncan

ACKNOWLEDGEMENTS

My personal thanks to Earl Mountbatten of Burma for so kindly writing the foreword to this book and his great and sincere interest in the plight of the Japanese prisoners-of-war at all times.

*

To the Imperial War Museum for supplying photographs of the entire Collection and giving consent to their reproduction in this book and also for their comment on the volume as a whole.

*

To my true friend and comrade Bill Duncan who had contributed his own feelings and opinions on this book.

*

To Lord Russell of Liverpool for his authoritative comment regarding the accuracy of my statements of Japanese behaviour to P.O.W.'s.

*

To the Wellcome Historical Medical Museum for their comments.

*

To my lifelong friend Eric Newman for his kind permission to include the sketch I made of him as a P.O.W. and for his loyal comradeship at all times.

*

To the family of 'Jock' Pearce for contributing all the drawings I did for him in Changi.

*

To the memory of a fine soldier, a great gentleman and my

true friend Major W. E. Gill for all his help and encouragement in the difficult years after the last war.

*

To all my many friends and comrades in the prisoner-of-war camps who helped and inspired me to produce my collection of paintings and eventually this book.

*

To Roger Chapman, my very good friend, who has made the publication of this piece of history possible.

THE ARTIST

Leo Rawlings was born in Birmingham on the 16th May, 1918. He suffered several serious illnesses as a child and showed little promise as a boy of ever being an artist, although he had great encouragement from his mother. The year that he won his first scholarship to the Central School of Art in Birmingham his mother died and his last bulwark of confidence departed.

He began his studies at the Mosely Road School of Arts and Crafts at the age of 11 where, feeling the loss of his mother probably more deeply than the average child might and owing to extreme nervous sensitivity (this same nervous sensitivity was to prove invaluable to his work in later years) his progress, according to those who taught him, was practically nil. His self-confidence was also marred by a serious speech defect which stayed with him until his late teens. The ultimate result was that, at the age of 13, his father was asked to remove him from the school by the then Headmaster as 'he would *never* make an artist'. His family moved to the North and made their home in Blackpool where he began to attend evening classes for as many subjects of art as he could cram in. In the day time he worked as a signwriter earning 5s. od. per week as a boy apprentice and six times a week he attended classes. During this time he passed various drawing and painting examinations and at the age of 17 was running his own one-man business as a scenic and display artist. There was great scope for his growing talents in Blackpool at that time.

Shortly after the Munich crisis he joined the Blackpool T.A. and, during the six months that followed, prior to the outbreak of war, trained as a Gunner/Signaller with the 137th Field Regiment R.A.

His Regiment was mobilised on the outbreak of war and for the next twelve months he was stationed in various camps in

England. During this time, apart from with his Unit, he became known as the Regimental Artist, producing many portraits of Officers and his own friends in the ranks; decorating many Officers' Messes with vivid, imaginary paintings of battles. Through the merits of his paintings in the Regiment, his Commanding Officer, Major W. E. Gill, brought his work to the attention of the late General Ironside.

In September, 1941, his Unit was posted overseas to support the garrison of Singapore. Within a few days of landing, the Japanese declared war. His Regiment was sent to the front line in Northern Malaya, and for the weeks that followed, until the capitulation of Singapore on the 15th February, 1942, they fought a continuous rearguard action with many desperate battles.

Amidst the battle and during the lulls in the fighting the artist managed to scribble a few details of the scenes around him. The rest he memorised being blessed with a photographic memory. Shortly after he was taken prisoner these drawings came to the notice of Lt. General Sir Louis Heath, who immediately commissioned him, unofficially, to keep accurate records from that time onwards of his experiences and those of his fellow prisoners-of-war, in order that as complete a pictorial dossier as possible could be accumulated of any war crimes committed.

General Heath loaned the artist his own personal Log Book of the Campaign, so that the drawings should be accurate and authentic. Having practically no paints with which to work, the artist used materials such as clay, root juices from plants etc., and made brushes from his own hair.

General Heath supplied him with a small quantity of drawing paper, and after this was used up, he painted on any paper material he could find; the backs of prison crime sheets stolen from Changi Jail, Singapore, and a crude type of Chinese rice-paper. Most of his paintings were executed when he himself was a very sick man in a jungle hospital. As they were completed the paintings were hidden in a self-constructed container made from an old stove-pipe, and buried in the earth beneath his bed, until the day of Freedom arrived.

Regarding the keeping of secret records and pictures of prison life – and atrocities – the Japanese had already issued an order that anyone found to be in possession of a camera, radio or even a diary, would be executed on the spot and indeed many who tried were. The artist owes it to the help and steadfast allegiance of many of his comrades (who kept watch for him whilst he worked) that these paintings were ever produced and retained, in British hands, as the only *complete* record of an entire theatre of war.

With the dropping of the Atomic Bomb in 1945 thousands of Allied prisoners' lives were saved. Leo Rawlings gathered up his paintings from their various hiding places and began the journey home to 'Blighty'.

Within a fortnight of arriving in England the artist, though still in poor health, took his collection of paintings to London with the burning desire to convey the awful truth to the people. But here, alas, he came up against apathy and indifference from many official quarters and it was not until 1946 that his collection of paintings began to be recognised for what they were. His first exhibition was organised by his ex-Commanding Officer, the late Colonel W. E. Gill, on the occasion when Blackpool offered him a one-man show in the Grundy Art Gallery. The attendance was staggering and from then on a series of exhibitions was held in various parts of the country, all in aid of war charities and deserving causes. Over £20,000 was raised during this time and the paintings received numerous civic honours and acknowledgements.

In 1958 Lord Russell of Liverpool produced his book *The Knights of Bushido* and in it appeared eight pages of reproductions of the original war paintings by Leo Rawlings. This book was reproduced in several other countries.

In 1964, although now in good physical health, the artist was beginning to get the effects of reliving his experiences in giving lectures and endless exhibitions. On his doctor's advice he decided to dispose of the collection. When consulted, Sotheby's of London thought them to be a most unique collection and a most valuable part of history and put a very high valuation figure indeed on them.

After a week's exhibition at the Artist's Own Gallery, London, from which the artist broadcast on B.B.C. and which was honoured by a visit from Earl Mountbatten of Burma, the collection was auctioned by Messrs. Wallis and Wallis of Lewes, the auction being televised by Southern T.V., preceded by a personal T.V. interview with the artist.

Many of the paintings were purchased by the Imperial War Museum, including photographic copies of every painting reproduced in this book.

INTRODUCTION

Leo Rawlings wrote this book simply because he damn well had to, not with any preconceived notions that he would make his fortune by so doing but with the desperation of deep mental conflict that was clouding and clogging his life. In his every day by day actions, his association with others around him, he saw a reflection of his former life as a prisoner of war under the Japanese. He developed manias for tiny, unimportant details that most people take for granted – such as possessing a horror for wasting even a crumb of bread, or a potato peeling. Anything that was even vaguely edible he watched with worried eyes, unable to accept that now he had all he needed as regards food, clothes etc. – and always secretly hoarding anything that looked as if it could one day be used to create something useful.

But it did not end there. For the first ten years of freedom, back in Britain, the reaction of want and starvation, cruelty beyond compare, and an ever present consciousness of death made itself felt daily and ricocheted around his mind in a mad, uncompromising whirl that had no beginning and no ending. It took a lot longer than those ten years, which inadvertently took an unhappy toll on those who came into his life during that period, before realisation of the origin of his mental torment took a tangible form and he was able to attack the cause constructively.

In the prison camp he had rarely, if ever, allowed things to get him down – mainly because of his belief in his spiritual guides and regular yoga practice which he had learnt from a fellow prisoner. But an all too rapid return to civilisation had dulled his sense of proportion on life as a whole; too much food, too much alcohol, too much everything, and from living as a low cast native for three and a half years the change was made too suddenly to be absorbed by one who literally lives by his emotions.

No later than four weeks after arriving home in this country he began a frenzied round of exhibitions of his prison camp paintings, bent on two things only – to tell the civilised world what war was really like and, if possible, to bring some financial help to his former comrades, many of them now physical and mental wrecks. So great was his desire to help others that his own health became secondary and, consequently, slowly degenerated. Nervous crack-ups followed, reducing his own financial position very often to a desperate situation.

At last, in a deep mental depression and heavily obligated in all directions, he followed the advice of his Doctor and allowed his paintings – the work that meant years of devotion and dedication – to be auctioned publicly. Although financially not only unrewarding but disastrous, the sale of the paintings seemed, for the time being at least, to have severed the chain that bound him to the past.

For a year he almost convinced himself that he had at last laid the ghost and, given time, would eventually regain a normal outlook on life. Slowly, however, the shadow that had lain across him drifted back until all his old fears and depressions were with him again. The reader shall not be bored by the actual effects of this new return to the pit of despair. Let it be sufficient to say that his private life was almost shattered beyond repair and he even at times contemplated removing himself from the physical scene for good. Like most artists or creative people he varied between his physical emotions and a deep spiritual need to express his feelings and prove to himself and all concerned that he was still unbeaten. Advice and criticism was showered upon him but once again a Doctor friend came up with a practical suggestion, in effect that he should write down all he could remember about his war and prisoner of war period and once and for all clear his subconscious of the horrors that still remained there. So it was that, purely to hold a mirror to his own soul and past, he commenced work on this book.

To some it would be difficult, if not impossible, to delve

back so far into circumstances they had desperately tried to forget, but every detail, almost every face, was still etched vividly in his memory and in eight weeks flat a task he had thought impossible had been achieved, written exactly in his own language without pretence of literary standards he did not possess and with no attempt to either distort or improve on the facts as he knew them to be. With the setting down of this vital period of his life the author's health began to improve steadily and although still carrying a deep concern and awareness for those who took part in those fateful years, his everyday life as a painter took an upward turn and assumed a more normal perspective.

With the completion of the writing many friends suggested that it should be made into a book as others may possibly profit from his experiences and apply the principles to their own lives. Almost reluctantly the author showed the manuscript, including the photographs of his war paintings, to the late Robert Pittman who, at that time, was Book Critic of the *Daily Express*. His verdict was that, in his opinion, such a book should be published as it contained not only an important piece of history but also showed the individual's ability to overcome adversity in many forms. Four years were to come and go before publication was to be achieved – years that were to be dogged by one refusal after another by publishers and agents. But firmly determined by now that it had all been worth while whatever happened, Leo battered away at every possible avenue that even remotely looked as if it could lead to eventual success in his aim to bring his own experiences before as wide a public as possible. Through constant press reports and articles by national and local newspapers a continual stream of requests for the book poured in. Everyone who read the master copy of the book acclaimed it as a masterpiece, and Film Producers saw it as a four million (£) enterprise. Twice it was literally accepted by Film Companies but each time delay and opposition bogged it down. Convinced beyond all doubt by now that the book would be well received and would sell well, the author, with the help of a good friend – Roger Chapman – launched the project. It is now left for the reader to be the final judge as to whether all that is set down and shown in this book has been a waste of time or a sincere contribution to history and humanity as a whole. Literary experts have criticised the manner in which the story has been presented. Publishers have even agreed to accept it on the condition that it was re-written by a ghost writer. But believing that the whole importance of the story lay in the fact that it had been an impulsive reaction based on a deep factual knowledge of a subject, Leo refused to have any alterations made. Certain of the illustrations also have been condemned by publishers as disgusting and obscene, but in the author's mind they were recorded accurately entirely from a medical and psychological viewpoint and are a vital contribution to what otherwise would have been just another war book. Every word and phrase has been subjected to the severest inspection by the author himself and only in the cause of honesty and truth has he allowed certain criticisms of authority to remain. No wilful attempt has been made to discredit any level of rank or file deliberately, or to unfeelingly cause distress to any friend or relative of deceased persons and the author sincerely apologizes for any unintentional slur or inference that is interpreted by any reader. Deep in his mind were, and still are, lasting memories of grave miscarriages of justice, very often carried out by those who were in a position of trust. The morale of the troops in action was very often sabotaged by well meaning but half trained leaders and, as prisoners, many men found they had two forces against them – the Japanese and their own administration. All these things happen in a war, and war is bad, but bad or good, it is always with us and man becomes a beast of the jungle bent on selfishness and destruction unless he allows his actions to be contained by a spiritual consciousness that must remain supreme at all times.

By his own experiences of war and peace Leo Rawlings has learned a deep and tolerant understanding of many people of the world, seeing his own struggles and defects as daily lessons to be self-learnt and used for future applications to problems yet to come.

CONTENTS

		Page
	Dedication	2
	Foreword	7
	Acknowledgements	15
	The Artist	17
	Introduction	21
	Prelude to War	27
1	THE MALAYAN CAMPAIGN	37
2	SLIM RIVER BATTLE 'KEDAH'	43
3	THE RETREAT CONTINUES	46
4	THE LAST DITCH. *Fall of Singapore*	51
5	THE BEGINNING OF THE LONG WAIT. *The trek up country*	59
6	THE RAILWAY CAMPS	67
7	BRIDGE BUILDING, THE 'RIVER KWAI'	74
8	MEDICAL. *Dysentery. Cholera. Vitamin Deficiency and its effects. Medical conditions. Ulcers. Other Tropical Diseases*	78
9	BACK TO SINGAPORE. *Japanese atrocities*	93
	Artist's Note	118
	Introducing Bill Duncan. *His valuable contribution to this document*	120

Lord Mountbatten's gracious foreword to this book is most highly valued by both Leo Rawlings and Bill Duncan and, as he was not directly involved with events related to in this book, he can in no way be held responsible for views expressed here.

PRELUDE TO WAR

Eleven o'clock Church Parade on a fateful Sunday morning in the year 1939. Along with the rest of my Regiment, the 137th Field Regiment, R.A., I sat in a pew of a Blackpool church and, with a feeling that was half jubilation and half dread, listened to the Vicar announce that this day, 3rd September, 1939, we were at war with Germany. An excited buzz swept the building as the full realisation of what had happened dawned upon us. We had all known it was coming. The events of the past year had slowly but irrevocably plodded their jack-booted trail towards the now obvious fact that at last someone was going to have to stop Hitler, the self appointed Chancellor of Nazi Germany, or try to prevent him from achieving his crazy aims at world domination.

Among the ranks of our little Regiment pride glowed on almost every face, an entire Territorial mob drawn from the many trades and professions of the town. We had answered the call to arms when the Munich crisis had loomed and from then on had trained vigorously and eagerly to become proficient in the use of field guns and their accoutrements. 'We'd show 'em', we thought to ourselves. 'No bloody Huns are landing in this country, not if we have anything to do with it!' Had we but known our pathetic lack of know-how and toughness, to say nothing of actual skill in the use of modern equipment as compared to the crack Divisions that were carrying out Adolf Hitler's plans, we may well have flinched and turned pale. But we did not know and as well for us that we did not, for much lay ahead of us that was to carve a bloody swathe through these mothers' sons of this happy seaside town – and turn the minds of many of those who were even to survive the ordeal of war.

Having been mobilised a week previously to the declaration of war, for the first few weeks or so most of us were billeted in our own homes as no other accommodation was available in the town (other than the Regimental Drill Hall which could only house Q.M. Staff and a guard of six men.) A truly amusing situation arose when we paraded for drill each day and during the afternoons either went swimming or carried out local route marches for an hour or two. We were then dismissed and sent home for the day to meet socially later in the evening in small groups to drink ourselves incapable or date the many eligible girls of the locality.

This happy state continued for some weeks until, finally, the Regiment was moved to Kirkham, a small village just outside Blackpool, and billeted in an old, condemned cotton mill, Brook Mill by name, rat infested and filthy. We were set to work to rehabilitate the place and, seeing the huge white-washed walls of the inside of the mill, I obtained permission to decorate these with enormous battle scenes of my imagination. The idea caught on and very soon I was ordered to extend my efforts to the creation of similar scenes in the Officers' and Sergeants' Mess. Eventually portraits of various Officers followed, much to the irritation of my Sgt. Major, a man whose only qualification for his post seemed to be his loud voice. Painting portraits meant being excused from duty and taken off guard detail of which he entirely disapproved and continually showed his feelings by putting me on guard or fatigue the moment my artistic efforts were completed. For the whole period of our stay in England I was the centre of a constant tug of war between officers who wanted portraits of either themselves or their wives, and Sergeants and Sergeant Majors who insisted that I was a serving soldier and should not be given such priority and privileges. Feeling myself to be the cause of constant trouble and dissentment and yet desperately feeling the need to express myself in paint when ever possible, I made various applications for a transfer to a Camouflage Unit or even the post of a war artist – something I had always wanted to be since a small boy. All my applications were turned down or dismissed out of hand but I never ceased to aim at this position whenever possible.

After a few months in Kirkham we were posted to Liverpool.

My own crowd, 350 Battery, were billeted in the slum area of Nile Street, a place ridden with dirt and decay and populated with the flotsam and jetsam of human life. An old school was our home for some weeks and during that time I became aware of the warm hearted people of Liverpool. As a whole their hospitality to our troops was overflowing and many of us were regularly entertained in local homes. Our various needs and desires being well catered for by the occupants and, in many cases, the daughters of the house in particular.

One such family, the Chambers, took me to their hearts for some reason and, having two lovely daughters, it was inevitable that a romance should develop between one of them and myself. Dorothy, the eldest girl, and I hit it off very well. She was a tall, dark, beautiful girl with two different coloured eyes, hazel and pale blue. This combination did nothing to mar her good looks and sweet disposition and we had a long and happy association until the Regiment finally moved away from the area.

Having painted most of the Officers in my Regiment by now, and, being on active war service as it was called, I had little time left to devote myself to drawing at all. But whenever I found myself on guard duty I would amuse myself by sketching pencil portraits of my fellow guards between shifts in the Guard room. This kept my hand in and I must have produced literally hundreds of such drawings as time went on.

About this time the Blitz on Britain's industrial towns was approaching its crescendo, and from the comparative safety of our sandbagged billets on Allerton Golf Course, we watched night after night as 'Jerry' droned overhead unloading his rain of death and devastation. The London Blitz has always had the limelight but Liverpool also had its full share of bombs, as the blazing docks could testify. Troops and civilians alike huddled together in air raid shelters or basements, watching grimly the picture of their homes and all they loved being blown to pieces.

In December, 1940 the whole Regiment was ordered to take up position as Depot Regiment at Lark Hill, Salisbury Plain, the Regiment's job being to train young officers from the

School of Artillery. This bleak, cheerless Plain, dotted only with the occasional house at that time, and bearing the symbol of the ancient Druids – Stonehenge – was to be our last stopping place in this country before the real test of our manhood was to come in distant lands overseas. During this year we were engaged in tireless training of all descriptions and for long hours each day, in every kind of weather, we carried out exercises and manoeuvres such as were expected we would encounter in Europe fighting the Nazis. Our ranks had now been injected with intake (mainly conscripts) from other regiments. Conscription now being at full blast, thousands upon thousands of men were drafted to the Plain to supplement and bring up to full war strength the units deployed there. During this time I contracted measles, the one and only case on the entire Plain. I was 'very' popular! I had it badly too which turned out to be a good thing eventually as it won me three weeks' sick leave and a spell in my home town Blackpool.

Upon my return to Lark Hill I was ordered to assist the Regimental Concert Party in its preparations for a farewell concert. I say 'farewell' because we had all suspected for some time that the hour was close for our departure overseas. Indeed many of us were impatient to be off as the life on the Plain had been irksome and boring. Being an experienced scenic artist also I was put in charge of the stage decor and enjoyed myself by revelling in paint again for some weeks. We had many good acts among our ranks including our Second in Command, Major Cary Outram who took upon himself the role of 'The Red Shadow', much to the amusement of many of us who knew he really fancied himself in the part. His voice was good though and he always drew a respectful if somewhat amused applause.

The show eventually took place and was a great success and a qualified excuse for a general 'booze-up' afterwards, at the expense of the officers.

Two weeks later it came. Embarkation orders were posted up on the notice board. We eagerly read the lists of names due to go overseas. Several of us had been struck off or left out owing to physical disability or age. Below eighteen or over forty-five years were, I believe the limits, but I saw my own name and a great thrill ran through me. 'This was it! Now to see some real action'. After a week of inoculations and check ups the Embarkation Leave lists went up and I found myself in the last batch to go home for seven days of leave before setting out on what was to be the greatest adventure of my life.

Very shortly, on a train going north from Euston Station, I sat in a compartment crowded with other troops who were also on Embarkation leave from other units. We discussed the probabilities of our destinations, although previously warned by our officers not to do so. 'Careless talk costs lives' was the slogan on posters everywhere but troops together will always talk, especially in the company of their own kind. Rumour had it that we were either going to America to train there for a special force to be used in invasion whenever that happened, or the Middle East where the Allies were being pushed back on all fronts. The conversation drifted off into other personal matters by the end of the journey and as dawn was breaking the train pulled into Blackpool South Station and I yawned a brief goodbye to my mates and caught a tram to my home in Kenilworth Gardens, South Shore. I let myself in with my key not wishing to disturb my Father and Stepmother who still slept, made myself a hot drink and decided it was a waste of time going to bed at 6.30 a.m. My Father had heard me however, and came down to share a cup of tea with me. 'Christ, I'm tired', I said, this being the first thing I could think of to say to him. He looked aghast at me and remonstrated on my language. 'Everybody says that in the army, Dad', I told him, but he preferred to make an issue of this slip on my part than to try to understand why I had said it. Not having been in the First World War himself he did not know the ways of soldiers. He was a good man but out of touch with real life as it was then and my leave was a mixture of complaints from him that I was going out every night, instead of spending my time with him, and indulging in a round of drinking with my old pals in the town. My lifelong friend Eric Newman was also on leave and we spent much of the time together, escorting various girls whenever possible. Although a normal youth in most ways

I had little success with girls at that age and practically no sex life at all, which is more than can be said for many of my more fortunate companions. I had much to learn of the gentle art of seduction.

The time came for my departure back to camp and one warm, sunny September afternoon I walked with my Father to catch a local tramcar to the station, having said goodbye to my Stepmother, whom I adored, earlier on. She had taken it badly having lost two brothers in the first war, but she was a brave woman and did her best to hold back her feelings. My army training had toughened me a lot and all I felt as I said cheerio to my Father was a rather exultant feeling of freedom of purpose. He too was a tough old bird and managed a cheery grin saying 'You will come back Leo, my boy. Carry yourself like a man at all times'.

On the train back to Lark Hill I flirted mildly with every girl I met as there were a lot of service girls also returning from leave. Suddenly time was running out, it seemed. Would I ever see this land again? A sickly fear came over me and I felt very afraid but fortunately the girl sitting opposite me un-crossed her legs at that moment and my mind was distracted to pleasanter thoughts which put my temporary cowardice out of my mind. 'Thank Heaven for girls', I thought later!

Almost as soon as I returned to camp, parades were held daily to issue tropical kit. Topees, khaki drill, great ugly shorts which let down to cover your knees at night to keep off mosquitoes – and mosquito cream which smelt like drainwater, to rub on your face and arms. Long sleeved shirts and various other accoutrements of tropical wear.

A week later all was ready to move out and, as we assembled on the Parade ground, the entire local population turned out to give us a good send off. Loaded down with kit but precious few small arms – one rifle between four men was all we could muster in the way of defensive weapons apart from the 25 pounders themselves with which my unit was armed – we set out. We had been told that artillery was miles behind the lines so we did not worry too much at our lack of arms.

We entrained for Liverpool and the following day went

aboard our troopship, the *Dominion Monarch*, a vessel of some 27,000 tons. The ship was part of a convoy which we were due to join later at sea. We stood off for about twelve hours before finally moving slowly up the coast. As the much loved Blackpool Tower came in sight a hush settled on the ship's company and literally frozen, emotionally, we stood in silent prayer that we would all see it again very soon. Many of us, we suspected, would not return to enjoy the good life again as we had known it, but we each hoped, I am sure, that it would not be us who died on a foreign shore. We cheerfully began singing our regimental songs to lift our spirits and soon settled down to life at sea.

The second day out we hit heavy weather and the *Dominion Monarch*, not being fully loaded, rolled and pitched like a cork. I was, fortunately, not to be sick but many men were and could not even eat the first class food provided by the navy. However, the weather soon improved and gave way to average conditions. We found our sea legs and, apart from light duties and parades of various kinds, found ourselves enjoying the trip – sunbathing and relaxing and almost feeling that 'this was the life after all'.

During this time a certain barrier seemed to develop between some of the Officers and men. The Officers did not mix at all socially with us and were very distant when on parade, trying, no doubt, to 'put us men in our place as serving soldiers' as some of them were heard to say. A certain Officer, who shall be nameless, adopted a snobbish superiority towards all and sundry and rumour had it he even had our rations cut by telling the Naval Cook aboard that the food was too good for the likes of us. To say we disliked him is an understatement. The day of advanced understanding between Officers and those in the ranks was yet to dawn. But most 137th Field Officers behaved decently to their men.

Our ports of call included Cape Town where we were met with a hospitality quite unknown to us before. The good people there just could not do enough for us and put their cars at our disposal and, in many cases, even their daughters to escort us around the beautiful city and take us on picnics to the

33

many beauty spots that abound in that wonderful land. Somewhat overwhelmed by the hot climate, vivid colours such as I had never dreamed of before, the bracing sea air and the generosity of the people of the Cape, I, for once, felt too relaxed and lazy to paint. Instead, a new world had opened up to me, a world of vital life, adventure and tropical splendour and even romance. I meant to absorb and enjoy every single second of it whilst it lasted. I had personally been adopted, for the four days shore leave allocated to us, by a big hearted Boer family who were blessed with a beautiful daughter called Eileen. A mere sixteen she was fully developed physically and full of vitality and charm. We seemed to fall in love at first sight and in the short time allowed us were never apart. Her grandmother, the one with the money (she owned a diamond mine), put it to me that if I could jump ship – in other words 'desert' – she would hide me until my ship had sailed, allow me to marry her grand-daughter and even set me up in business as an artist. Many times since I have wondered if I made the right decision by refusing, which, I have to admit, I did with much sorrow. Eileen and I swore to write to each other but fate decided otherwise and the cameo ended there and then.

We left Cape Town with tearful regret, barely a dry eye amongst us as, lining the ship's rails, we waved farewell to what had been a fairyland episode in our lives.

By now we knew our destination, Singapore, to support the garrison already there, but as we had been told before the chance of any fighting was extremely unlikely as, apart from being a stronghold Naval Base, the Japs could only come by sea and a battery of heavy naval guns entirely covered the approach to the Island. The journey continued onwards calling only at Columbo, Ceylon, for a few hours and then south to Singapore. Our convoy had now grown in number to over thirty ships of all kinds and when two Focke-Wulf German long range bombers made a skirmishing attack on us they received a hot reception and made off. Our naval escort efficiently disposed of a brief submarine attack also and we seemed to bear a charmed life. After roughly five weeks from leaving Liverpool we sailed into the Straits of Singapore.

Short, stumpy little islands and mainland preluded our approach to the docks, swathed in early evening mist. Lights twinkled from a thousand huts and private houses and the aromatic aroma of burning sandalwood, tropical dried fish and a hundred other strange smells intoxicated our nostrils. 'No wonder it was called the glamorous East', I thought. What a fantastic way to spend a war! The troopships took their allotted places along the dockside and eventually, in mid evening, we disembarked to the sound of a military band playing on the dockside. But here the civilian reception was different – a hell of a lot different. The local whites made it painfully clear that we were only common soldiers sent to the garrison then already an impregnable fortress. There was no official welcoming speech or even a brief greeting from the Governor. Just a quick N.A.A.F.I. meal and then a long march to entrain for up country to an army camp situated near the village of Kajang, Malaya. We had arrived and what lay ahead was anybody's guess!

The night journey by train was punctuated only by occasional halts in sidings and the incessant drone of mosquitoes. Daubed in anti-mosquito cream, tired, sweating like pigs and trying to catch a brief nap, our morale had slipped somewhat. No longer did we feel like well trained, high spirited troops about to occupy an impregnable fortress under idyllic conditions but just a bunch of weary, travel stained boys playing at soldiers. Quite suddenly the gilt had gone off the ginger bread. Although personally still rather enjoying the situation, in a strange kind of way, I now began to feel a certain foreboding that perhaps this would not turn out to be quite the piece of cake some of us contemplated.

Arriving at Kajang as dawn broke the following morning, we left the train in a gully at the approach to the station and marched through rubber plantations to the Camp of wooden huts set on a hill overlooking the village. The sky was a mass of brilliant colours – gold, silver, purest of blues and deep purple horizon clouds splitting apart like enormous fingers breaking from a handclasp.

We settled quite comfortably into our new home and got

down to work maintaining trucks, guns, stacking ammunition and a few days passed in this manner. The days were busy, food was good and apart from the heat to which we were rapidly becoming accustomed, life seemed good again. The nights, full of surrounding jungle noises, including crickets which never stopped for one second, were cool and sleep-inducing. But this was not to last.

One such night about 10 p.m. the crickets did stop. A deathly hush fell on the camp and it occupants whispered to each other in the half light, 'Listen, the crickets have stopped. Sounds queer without 'em.' Similar comments followed and then we heard it – the drone of plane engines approaching high overhead. 'It's only the R.A.F. out on patrol, I expect', said someone. The sounds passed and we thought no more of the incident until the following morning. As we lined up for breakfast an excited buzz swept the camp. 'Singapore was bombed last night by the Japs. Christ,' we thought 'they're going to have a go at us. Bastards!' By midday tiffin (lunch) we knew the worst. The Imperial Japanese Army had been allowed to come right through Thailand with full co-operation of the Thai Government and were heading for Northern Malaya. But more was to come – a task force had been sighted by a Sunderland Flying boat off the North East coast of Malaya, probably aiming for Kota Bahru where our further-most air strip was situated.

By tea time we were under orders to move out to take up defensive positions in the area of Jittra, Northern Malaya and to hold the main road leading from there down to Singapore. All was instant haste and preparation to move and by dawn the following day we were heading North with all speed.

CHAPTER I

THE MALAYAN CAMPAIGN

December, 1941. .... Confident, eager but raw in experience of war, unblooded and possessing a total lack of training in jungle warfare in particular, we sailed blithely into action against a canny, vicious, cruel and highly experienced jungle fighter, the Japanese. Having fondly imagined when in Britain that we would soon be in France fighting the conventional war of our forefathers as in World War I, based largely on the hair raising stories told by 'old sweats' in the Barrack Room, it had come as something of a shock when we discovered ourselves embarked to the unknown mysterious East. As one old Reservist was heard to remark 'You don't know how lucky you are, lads. Lots of sun, lots of booze, lots of women. You won't even get a fighting war'. And we believed him – at least, some of us did.

The assault on the Peninsular commenced with the Japanese attack on Kota Bahru on the North Eastern Coast of Malaya. The odds against us were calculated by some senior British Officers as being five to one. Japanese troops consisted of roughly three to four divisions of highly trained assault troops, very well armed indeed with automatic weapons in great numbers. British and Allied forces numbered something like one and a half divisions of Infantry and light artillery in support, including a small number of mortar positions not too amply stocked with ammunition. Bitter fighting commenced and continued for some time. Wave after wave of Japanese were thrown back but still they came on. Assault craft crammed to bursting point poured an ever increasing flood of yellow fanatics against the defenders and sweating, blood-stained British and Indian Infantry fired until barrels of rifles and guns became almost too hot to function. Finally, leaving a beach full of dead and dying Japanese, and many of our own numbers amongst them, we were ordered back to defend the vital air strip further inland. Seizing the initiative the Japanese now increased their pressure along the whole area of attack, following up with heavy air attacks by carrier-based planes on the 'drome' itself which finally fell to the invaders.

Throughout the action of landing these troops and in taking the Air Strip the Jap suffered many heavy losses. British losses were considerable but not as heavy by comparison to those of the Japanese who flung themselves into battle with fanatical fervour, screaming and shouting their war cries and making the night hideous. Finally, our troops were ordered to fall back to prepared positions and consolidate.

With the influx of the Japs into Kota Bahru terrified native civilians poured out of the area, dragging screaming children along the one and only road down country. Either carrying their pitiful belongings and what food they could cram onto bullock carts, or even on their own shoulders. The situation resembled the days of Dunkirk as British and Indian Army lorries eased their way along the column of refugees. The Asiatic down the ages has usually accepted upheaval and catastrophe with a certain fateful calm but to these poor wretches who had probably lived a peaceful existence in these parts for many years, the shock of losing their homes was too much for them and they even fought each other to escape the horror developing behind them down the now crowded road.

By this time the Oil Dump in Kota Bahru had been set alight – either by shell fire or by our own troops in an effort to rob the Jap of any supplies possible. Japanese dive bombers were active all the time and civilians and troops alike were shot at. Some of the Indian drivers of Allied trucks panicked and drove their vehicles completely off the road into the paddy fields bracketing the highway.

The Blackpool Regiment, 137th Field, 25 pounders, were now in action only a matter of hours after the Japanese had effected their successful initial landings. For the greater part of our first day, C Troop, the one in which I served as a Signaller, fired almost continuous barrage and harassing fire at Jap concentrations some few miles further up the road. About 4 p.m. there seemed to be a lull in the fighting and the sweating gunners rested briefly by their guns.

We were not to rest for long however. Reports came in that Jap Infantry was infiltrating through our lines and that the main front position held by Indian Troops, Punjabis and Sikhs, had been penetrated. To this day we do not have a clear picture of what really happened. It is sufficient to say that masses of Allied Infantry of all kinds came flooding down the road in shocked and shattered condition – obviously completely spent. We heard rumours that these troops had held the line for over four days under continual fire – and they looked it! Our guns immediately took up position on the road to offer covering fire and kept this up until most of our Infantry were clear.

Meanwhile, off the North East coast, the fine ship H.M.S. *Prince of Wales* along with her sister ship, *The Repulse*, had been sunk just as they were racing to intercept the Jap landings then taking place. Had these capital ships been successful in their mission, and had they been covered by adequate air support as were most Japanese vessels, it could have been a different story – but there is nothing clear in the way of news on the subject which suggests that the operation was carried out in a realistic manner. But that was another story. The *Prince of Wales* was attacked by 200 Jap aircraft – mostly carrier based – and subjected to one of the most fantastic and vicious attacks in Naval history. This action was described to me in laborious detail by six of the survivors whom I later met in Singapore at a hospital there. The details of the painting may give grounds for criticism but I am assured that the general atmosphere and ferocity of the situation is accurate. This gallant ship and her crew fought until they could fight no longer and many of her brave sailors were trapped in the red hot blazing hulk and finally went down with her. A few, a very few, were later picked up by Jap naval craft, and after being subjected to much cruel treatment and very little medical attention, were brought in to Singapore after the capitulation. These men were in a dreadful state and it was some time before they recovered sufficiently to recount the action.

And as practically our total naval support wallowed on the sea bed of the now Japanese dominated ocean, I imagine exultant Nippon officers drank their Emperor's health, congratulating themselves on a campaign that appeared to be a foregone conclusion.

But on the road to Singapore the defences were stiffening. Jittra had been a blow but considering that our total strength was in the region of one and a half divisions at that time, as against the Japs three to four divisions, perhaps we had not done too badly, against trained jungle fighters at that.

Now all efforts were being made to collect our forces and establish a new line. Columns of vehicles and guns lumbered South through the burning streets of Alor Star and Ipoh where evidence of heavy bombing and shelling was still apparent. Corpses filled the drains and wreckage littered the roadway. The aroma of dead flesh was everywhere, the first we had encountered, mixed in with the smell of Chinese and Indian foodstuffs gone rotten. Over everything hung the phantom of portending evil, an evil so great and yet hardly begun. Allied Infantry patrols probed the shadowed streets seeking some sign of the advancing Nips but the Jap, fearing ambush, usually waited for daylight before venturing into a new area, and then he came in force.

The Jap had struck so hard in his initial advance down country that many courageous Indian Regiments, namely Sikhs, Garwalis, Punjabis, etc., all led by British Officers, had been cut off from the main body of troops. Hating the Nip with a fanatical fervour, matched only by Nip himself, they had stuck grimly to their positions. Lines of communication had been cut in many cases and consequently the order to withdraw had never reached them. Finally, when their white Officers realised the true situation they were ordered to disengage the enemy in order to save lives. Carrying their wounded they made their way back towards our fast retreating line, often making wide detours to avoid capture. The quality of these Indian troops was never in question. They fought magnificently but few had seen any great action prior to the Malayan Campaign and were certainly not highly experienced in Jungle warfare as was the Nip.

It is necessary at this point to mention that, prior to the

commencement of hostilities, all troops had been lectured on the almost impossibility of the Jap attacking us on the right flank. British Intelligence, so authority told us, was convinced that no attack could or would be made from this direction, as many miles of impenetrable jungle would make progress impossible. Unknown to British Intelligence Jap fifth column supporters had spent almost two years prior to the war cutting secret roads through these jungles, and by using these roads the Nip constantly cut off our retreat, even bringing armoured columns to bear on us in some profusion. Throughout the entire campaign treachery and sabotage was rife amongst some of the local inhabitants, with the exception of the Chinese. These wonderful people helped and encouraged our troops wherever possible. A favourite touch of the saboteur was to place large banana leaves shaped like an arrow head in clearings and on the roadways, pointing directly at our troop concentrations and gun positions. It was then a simple matter for the Nip dive bomber to blast us out of existence. Lines of washing pointing in our direction were also used.

Probably the greatest and most feared of all native troops was the Ghurkha, the little man with the big heart. Quaint and sometimes comical in their ways, and utterly devoted to their white officers once that officer had proved himself a man of courage and character, and entirely without fear of anything visible or invisible. On several occasions our guns were fortunate in having them on the left flank in action and combined with the immortal Jocks on our right we were impregnable as far as the Jap infantry attacks went. Johnnie, as he was affectionately known to us gunners, was held in something akin to awe by his Indian comrades and in utter terror by the Nips. I have it on top rank evidence that on certain occasions during the jungle war these brave little men would fade away into the night towards the enemy lines. Armed only with their famous Kukri, they would await the coming of the enemy or even seek him out on his own ground, slaying silently and mercilessly until they themselves fell. There are many, many such stories of their heroism and devotion to duty. I have personally seen them almost cry like babies when ordered to retreat. To retreat from an enemy, no matter what the odds, is considered almost an insult and many Ghurkas even considered it damaging to their ancestry.

As the ground fighting flared and simmered and flared again, as the Nip threw overwhelming forces into the attack, strafing and dive bombing our tired but stubborn defences, our air force, what there was of it, struck back. Shortly after Christmas, 1941, twelve planes of the Australian Air Force Wildebeasts and Albacores, hit at Jap transports landing troops near Endau, north east coast of Malaya. Many direct hits were registered and great damage might have been sustained by the Japanese had not the appearance of some sixty Zeros suddenly taken place. Against such great odds these pathetic old kites had no chance whatsoever and all but one gallant old wreck were shot down. The surviving pilot, with his left leg shot off at the knee and a dead observer behind him, somehow managed to make his drome and land his plane. He described this incident to me from an adjoining hospital bed during the last week of the fighting on Singapore island.

We saw very little of modern R.A.F. planes. Fifty Hurricanes were sent out from the U.K. but in the face of total Jap air supremacy, those that did fly had little effect.

CHAPTER 2

SLIM RIVER BATTLE 'KEDAH'

The New Year of 1942 was to be one of the most momentous of our young lives. Few of us had envisaged our proud little Regiment being in the centre piece of one of the most significant, if not the biggest, campaigns of World War II. Such was the case however, and barely had we finished wishing each other a Happy New Year and a turn of the war in our favour, when Jap attacked again in force. Now that he held Kota Bahru Drome and all the surrounding coastline, nothing was simpler than for his troops to flood ashore in their thousands. Better armed, and with a jungle 'know how' far surpassing our own, he marched tirelessly and relentlessly forward – the goal – Singapore!

In the early dawn of a Sunday morning, with light mist covering his attack, he trundled three columns of tanks down the main Kedah road. Our Infantry put up a great show in an attempt to hold him, but after several hours of bitter fighting Jap broke through, leaving several wrecked tanks behind him.

At this point I must truthfully say that, in the opinion of Lt. Gen. Heath and Officers, much of the Jap advance could have been withheld for a longer period had our forces been highly organised in an efficient manner. Sad to say, this did not seem to be so. One reason why, I believe, the Malayan Campaign has been hushed up for so long. And in Government circles, just a dirty story – dishonourable, even – but not to the O.R.'s, for whom the ever present order was to do – and die! This they did, bless 'em.

The Jap tanks eventually reached the guns and blew hell out of them. Many courageous Gunners defied death to engage on 'open sights' but to no avail. Nip was too much for us. Blasted out at ground level, bombed and strafed from the air, chaos reigned as the little yellow men grinned their way into another victory.

Speaking as a Gunner myself, it may be thought that I have shown something of a bias in that direction – this I have endeavoured not to do, but one fact remains that must be mentioned. Had it not been for the tireless and accurate shooting of practically all Gunner Regiments the Jap advance would have been even swifter. Sometimes ribbed by the P.B.I. as having a safe job, this was certainly not so in Malaya.

It was at most times difficult to say where the enemy lay, or from what angle he would attack. He watched our gun flashes at night as we barraged him and beat hell out of us at dawn with planes, mortars and machine gun fire. Almost two whole Batteries of guns of the 137th R.A. were lost at Slim River and the survivors of this lightning hit and run attack (including some infantry units) were scattered into the surrounding jungle without food or supplies, many seriously injured, and left to make their own way back to our fast retreating line as best they could.

For several days these men, a mixture of ranks and units braved unmentionable horrors, sleeping rough at all times in the treacherous jungle, starving, crying with pain and disease, racked by dysentery and other charming side effects of their harrowing experience. Hardly daring to move out in the open by day for fear of Jap spotter planes or Jap Infantry, they travelled mainly by night, often losing what little equipment they still possessed in swamps and heavy undergrowth. A good friend of mine, Bert Wright, Batman to Lt. Col. Holme, C.O. of my own Regiment, lost his life as a result of this shambles. The Colonel (a fine man) was also killed in action prior to the attack. Liaison having broken down within the Regiment as a result of this catastrophe, the Jap attack was unexpected and now the survivors plunged wildly on into an unfriendly terrain, zigzagging from course to course, path to path and missing their way continually. Around precipices, through barbed bamboo thickets, across raging rivers and at all times scorched by a fierce tropic sun. Many lost their reason before their lives. Here, at last, was the beginning of the great test. A man was judged by how much he helped his comrades. Some fell by the way in more ways than one. Several fell into Jap hands and were executed on the spot, others tortured or burnt alive. The lucky ones made it to Kuala Lumpur to be imprisoned in the Jail there as prisoners of war.

There were the odd few who struggled on into friendly Chinese villages. Villages which had already suffered at the hands of Jap troops passing through, Japs who had hung their flags there and several innocent Chinese along with them. Even so, our brave Chinese friends defied discovery of their actions again by feeding these shattered remnants of a once proud army, rested them for a while and then set them on what they believed to be a safe road towards our own lines.

Of the Chinese I can speak nothing but good. They were brave, devoted and kindly people to whom treachery was unknown. Many times they risked their lives for us – and died for it.

CHAPTER 3

THE RETREAT CONTINUES

As the flare of Slim River died down, the Allied troops took stock of themselves, licked their wounds, and prepared to make yet another stand. The Australians – the tough, rugged, hard living, hard swearing diamonds that they were, and still are, hit at the Jap whenever they saw him, ruggedly defending every inch of their ground. Sometimes even fighting back to back in rubber plantations as Jap hemmed them in. To pin-point Regiments is not possible, either in praise or criticism, nor is that my intention, but to give an as accurate as possible general view of what took place. There were undoubtedly acts of cowardice, there always are in every war, but these were far outweighed by the main body who did their best against fearful odds. Very rarely did accurate news of the war come through to us. We fought as in a kind of 'limbo', always believing that eventually massive reinforcements would arrive to save the day. Unaware that our total sea support had gone to the bottom, and what troops were being hastily drafted to our help would arrive far, far too late, we were fast becoming the first forgotten army.

Communications between Command and Units were forever breaking down or being disrupted, either by constant enemy action or the effect of the rubber trees which made radio communication more than difficult – at times, impossible. Quite often we Signallers used existing telephone cables and tapped in on the wire. On two occasions I was operating on such a network when, to my horror, I heard Jap voices. Unknown to us both Jap and Allied Signallers had both tapped in on the same cable, proving that our front line as such had become somewhat flexible to say the least.

Hastily disconnecting my phone I informed my Officers and a maintenance party left at once to make new arrangements.

There being no one at my post who understood Nipponese, no advantages could be taken of the situation as regards interpreting the enemy activities in that area. The 'Bashers', as Signallers were named, were constantly in demand day and night in the foulest conditions, having to go out and repair broken telephone cables. So short of weapons and particularly small arms was the Army that in some artillery units one rifle between two men was a luxury. Signallers often went out unarmed. I carried a ·38 pistol which I had bought privately in England prior to embarkation. Known as the suicide squad in World War I, the sons of those men lived up to their forefathers' reputation to get the line through at any cost.

The illustration shows a small maintenance party of 88th Field Regiment, R.A., repairing a broken line under shellfire. One of their number was killed as a result of enemy action but showing great presence of mind and devotion to duty the remaining two signallers eventually made the line good again.

It was very rare that we stayed in any position longer than forty-eight hours, more often than not we would be ordered into a new 'hide' in the Rubber plantations either to reform and have a brief rest or commence harassing fire on the enemy through gaps in the trees and within an hour or so be moved out again as a Jap encircling movement took place behind us. He would land a small attack force from the sea on the West Coast and cut the roads behind us. Only the valiant efforts of the Infantry and R.A. combined would succeed in extricating us from certain annihilation. But in many cases those in command of us preferred to stage a 'strategic withdrawal' to a stronger position and establish a new 'line'. Being inexperienced in these new methods of Jungle warfare, they failed to realise that in such a country as Malaya this manoeuvre was almost impossible. Grimly they clung to the antiquated ideas of 1914–18 and I do believe hypnotised themselves into thinking that *one* such line would at least hold the Jap attack. Many brave men died before they were finally proved wrong and withdrawal after withdrawal took place, day after day, night after night, often through heavy monsoon weather.

Signallers have already been mentioned I know, but apart

from their normal duties of line laying through swamp, jungle, under fire and a hundred other difficult conditions, there was another side to the life in action of a 'Basher'. In many ways he had to be a 'Jack of all trades'. He could be called upon to perform duties way out of his area and qualification, from Bren Gunner, Anti-tank action and serving on the 25 pounders. Thirty-six hours non-stop duty was nothing in those days of man shortage and confusion. Whilst a man serving on the gun would quite often sleep by it between firing, a Signaller could finish a long turn of duty at Observation Post or Command Post and be put straight on guard. This was not victimisation, though thought so by many men, but usually a necessity due to our low numbers. It was just hard luck on the 'Basher'. In spite of these impositions the 'Basher' gave a damn good performance of all his duties – and usually managed to grin about it.

Whilst we up country were plugging away at the Jap with all we had, down country panic and confusion were rife. The native population, many terrified out of their wits – but others secretly welcoming their new Jap master to be – were dispersing in all directions. Some into the hills away from the active combatants and others towards Singapore. Allied troops in reserve positions were organising evacuation of civilians and supplies to the island of Singapore and Johore Bahru. Sick and wounded troops and civilians were loaded on to Red Cross trains for transport south. These stations soon became constant targets for Jap planes and usually any train bearing a Red Cross came in for special attention. The pathetic absurdity of panic evacuation still leaves a somewhat humorous flavour in my memory. Pompous officials who had been little Gods in charge of pin point villages insisted on their most ridiculous intimate possessions being taken along on trains already overloaded with women and children. They were a cult of whisky swilling civilians, some from tin mines and rubber plantations, who found it impossible to believe that their reign of minute power had ended. These unfortunate people held on to their imagined authority to the bitter end, little realising the fate already in store for them.

From the very first moment of the beginning of the battle for Malaya and Singapore until the last shot had been fired Japanese planes dominated the skies above us. The state of nervous tension from which many ex-servicemen still suffer today began in those early days of the war in the East when to put your head out of an already wrecked building or a camouflaged 'hide' was to court disaster. All day long the yellow wasps droned overhead, searching out troops and civilians alike, mercilessly and without quarter, ignoring Red Crosses on field ambulances and those boldly displayed outside Hospitals. I was in three different hospitals, far behind the lines, which were bombed and strafed unceasingly. The Indian troops were a light Mountain Gun Regiment moving from one position to another. Though bombed and machine gunned they returned fire with Bren and Lewis guns and succeeded in downing one of their attackers. The bombed and shell shattered villages we passed through day-by-day had the pathetic look of suddenly unwanted and dying creatures that only yesterday had throbbed with the life and laughter of their inmates. But now, with their life's blood ebbed and blasted away, they hung their mantles of telegraph wires and broken tiles like hair on a long dead skull.

The Campaign was now in something like its eighth week and Units were so internamed and mixed up that Artillery, Infantry and Indian troops of all denominations were quite often acting as a complete temporary unit. Whole regiments had been almost obliterated, cut to pieces or disbanded by the infiltrating Jap, and there were several occasions when Gunners, caught on the hop by a burst through of Japs, would fix bayonets and, supported by a motley mob of allsorts, charge the little yellow beasts. Jap Officers wielding Sumari swords, screaming their battle cry, would cut and slash in all directicns. The cries of attacking Nips is something I can never forget, rather like demons advancing from Hell, as indeed they were, to us. There may have been ordinary, brave Japanese soldiers to whom the massacre of unarmed men and women, not to say children was a disgusting and frightful act. If there were, I met them not, nor did any man I knew out there. The Jap as a jungle fighter was brave, this I grant. But rather a fanatical bravery of heavy odds on his side. In a straight fight of even odds, he was no better than any other soldier. Rather less, as the average Jap or Korean had little intelligence or individualism.

Yong Peng, where Captain Alan Grime, 137th Field Regiment, R.A., bravely distinguished himself in action, was probably the last main stand by Allied troops of any account before the withdrawal to Johore and finally Singapore. My own Unit, C. Troop of 350 Battery, 137th Field Regiment, R.A., held a gun position for four days. Partly hidden by banana trees, our Command Post in a small planter's house, we fired an almost continuous barrage on a variety of targets. Heavy supplies of ammo were piled high behind the guns and the intention was, we were told, to make a big stand here at last. Our spirits climbed a little at this news. At last, we told ourselves, we were digging our heels in. Our rejoicing was, as usual, short lived. At dawn on the 4th day heavy attacks by dive bombers blasted us out of our position. D. Troop on the other side of the road caught it most receiving severe casualties. It is an action I well remember. As the exit became obvious we piled all the ammo which lay around onto trucks and shot off down the road. Sitting on top of a stack of live shells, I clung on as our truck driver, Roy Stansfield, with great bravery, drove right through a section of road that was a sea of flame, caused by a burning gun limber set alight by a bomb. It did not occur to me at the time that one spark could well have blown us skywards.

CHAPTER 4

THE LAST DITCH – FALL OF SINGAPORE

With Yong Peng and the surrounding areas in the hands of the enemy, large quantities of our artillery gone, badly short of vital supplies and in many cases living off hard rations, the Army, such as it had now become, limped its unhappy way the last few miles to Johore Bahru and Singapore. I was among those billeted in the Sultan of Johore's Palace, now stripped of its former glitter and wealth. A lull had fallen on both sides and we had temporarily stopped to bind our wounds and take stock of the situation. Speculation was rife. Many thought we would be evacuated as at Dunkirk but where were the ships? Jap ruled the air, and very definitely the sea also. Lord Wavell had arrived, they said, to demand that we fight on to our last bullet. 'Will he stay with us?' went the question. He did not. Obviously the good General saw the writing on the wall and had orders to report back to H.Q., wherever that was now, with Jap holding most of the Pacific.

Four days later we left Johore and, blowing a hole in the Causeway connecting the mainland to the Island, we dug in on Singapore. The Jap lost no time in building a rough bridge but his first sally across fell victim to a terrific artillery barrage.

Making numerous attempts to invade the Island, each time with heavy casualties to himself, in spite of air supremacy, Jap eventually succeeded in swarming ashore via the mangrove swamps that cover the Island at various points. Shell fire from both sides was now increasing greatly and this, added to incessant blanket bombing by Jap, made life hell for all and sundry. The civilian population caught most of this as they were in exposed areas.

Over all the Island now hung the spectre of defeat. Thoroughly exhausted men, fighting as in a nightmare, trigger happy and gun shocked, lived each day as their last. The battery of huge 18 in. Naval guns covering the Singapore Straits, – thought to be the only approach from which an attack could come – proved useless, though superhuman efforts by Gunners did eventually turn one round to fire back up the Mainland. The screech of its shells travelling overhead at twenty minute intervals sounded like an express train hurtling through a station. Its actual effect on the enemy was little but it did boost our failing morale somewhat – at least, for a time.

The last week of fighting on the Island of the Lion – as the Chinese called Singapore – was a week I will never forget to my dying day. Never did men fight so hard or so well and never did it seem so much in vain. If V.C.'s had arrived by the box load they would not have been sufficient to honour the hundreds of acts of individual bravery and personal sacrifice that was the order of the day. Not just fighting men but medical officers, orderlies and women nurses, American, British and Australian, who defied hellish bombing and strafing to attend the sick and dying. I was in hospital during this time for acute septic throat and Jungle sores which covered my hands and arms making it almost impossible for me to hold even a cup. But around me were beds full of shattered and dying men in far worse condition than myself.

The building shown in the centre of my drawing was an improvised Hospital. Many times we were hit by bombs and shells as the planes droned overhead day and night. At times it was impossible to hear a shouted word as the bombs rained down upon us. Weeks after, in P.O.W. camp, I found a holiday snap of the exact spot I have shown and drew a reconstructed impression of what I felt had happened. I later inspected the same area whilst on a working party and the state of the buildings convinced me that I had not been far wrong in my deduction.

The painting 'Sinking of the *Empress of Asia*' depicts an attempt to land what could have been vital reinforcements to our failing cause, had they arrived in time. Known as the 3rd Corps and containing some seasoned and unseasoned troops, they came in a variety of ships including the *Empress of Asia*, a slow moving old tub long since past her prime. Escorted mainly by Destroyers she was a sitting duck for the Jap planes who screamed down on her and her convoy. She sank, blazing, in the Straits, many men going down with her. Never was an effort made to lead to so little for no sooner had the remnants of the 3rd Corps landed than many of them were taken prisoner. Some troops did, in fact, go into action but were cut to pieces almost as soon as they engaged the enemy. Being short of much of their equipment and ammunition they had little real chance to distinguish themselves but certain Infantry Units, the Leicesters amongst them, put up a terrific stand suffering heavy casualties themselves for their pains. During the campaign such great fighters as the Gordon Highlanders, Argyl & Sutherland Infantry and many others from 'Scotland the Brave' distinguished themselves beyond question and carried on their great tradition. Such was the situation on Singapore Island with the Japanese closing the net around us. Tokio must have rattled its chopsticks with joy at the prospect of such a fine, fat prize – soon to be theirs.

But the final victory that was fated to be Japan's was yet not quite won, even though it must have appeared so to their front line troops. Despite their constant and methodical air raids, consisting usually of 150 planes at a time in waves of about 25, what pathetic little Air Force we still possessed – an odd Hurricane or Brewster Buffalo, (a plane quite unsuited to tropical conditions) – hurled themselves valiantly at the great massed armadas which even scorned fighter escort. To the everlasting credit of those of the R.A.F. that were left to fight with us, though many had already been flown to Java and were P.O.W.'s already, they did their bloody best to make every bullet fired count and find a mark on some Nip pilot. Such was the Nip air mastery during the last days of fighting that a Japanese Observation Balloon drifted lazily on high over Johore Bahru, engaged in spotting our activities and confident in its own safety. The day before Singapore fell an exultant Jap fighter pilot commenced writing 'Surrender' in smoke lettering across the sky but he exulted once too often however, a tiny silver speck bearing red, white and blue markings fell on him out of the sun and he rejoined his forefathers.

On the ground, desperate and terrifying as the situation was, I felt a strange calm settle on myself and many others around me. We knew this was it! But I never heard one single man utter complaint or express fear. Rather a stoic fatalism had set in. Gunners and others ventured into the inferno of a burning ammunition dump to rescue much needed shells to keep the guns firing. Though every man on this job carried himself like a hero, I heard of no decorations as a result of it. The dump had been occupied first by us, taken by the Jap and then retaken by British Infantry and thereafter it was under constant bombardment by the Nip. It was a blazing hell of exploding ammunition of all calibres. Burnt out trucks and an ammunition train littered the area, spewing out of their shattered sides every conceivable type of weapon fodder. The heat was fantastic and men's skin blistered as they drove in. How their own trucks failed to blow up is one of those unexplainable mysteries of war. In spite of these difficulties the Gunners retrieved large supplies of vital gun food and kept the guns blazing away at the Jap ceaselessly by day and by night. Firing by relays they slept by their guns for fitful breaks, roused themselves when their brief rest was over and continued their barrage with bleary, bloodshot eyes.

Singapore itself was by now a mass of burning houses, buildings and warehouses. A waterway that runs through the middle of the City was flanked by numerous supply dumps containing oil and petroleum etc. Shell fire had been heavy in that area and had consequently set some of these on fire. The burning oil flowed down the banks into the water and, fanned by an evening breeze, it drifted through the City, a lake of fire burning all in its path. Cantonese boatmen and their terrified families fought to save their pathetic sampan homes, many being burnt alive. Sporadic fire from Nip snipers added to this satanic scene and Jap planes took advantage of the glare to pinpoint targets with well placed bombs. Many times during the Campaign through the eyes of the artist I had looked in wonder on many vivid scenes but to me now this was terrifyingly, magnificently horrible. The element of fire in its dreadful extermination of the human ant – as such all we mere earthlings are.

The last two days I spent in Raffles Theatre which had been turned into a front line casualty arena. Arena is true, for this was a battle ground in itself. The Gladiators were our wonderful Nurses and Doctors, mainly Australian and American but a few British, who defied certain death a hundred times a day to dash out through a sea of machine gun fire, mortar fire and bombs to rescue fallen troops and civilians. These magnificent women carried out their merciful work in the face of hell itself, with a calm detachment one expects and too often takes for granted. One American Sister never seemed to run out of humour. Her commentaries on everyday happenings were an education in themselves; full of vitality she seemed tireless, never ceasing to try to keep our minds off the inevitable. She was even taking bets of £100 to 1s. that the Jap wouldn't take Singapore. A sombre and tragic indignity lay in store, however, for her and all her flock of angels. They were eventually shipped out on the last boat to leave the Island. But on reaching Java they were captured by the Nip and were ordered to wade out into the sea. There they were machine gunned to death. In this way Japan honoured the Geneva Convention!!

And now, at last, the feared day had arrived. Feared? Disbelievingly, yes, for did any of us really believe it could happen? Would not some great Allied sea Armada suddenly 'hove to' on the horizon, blasting the Jap out of the water and hurl a load of crack Marines up the beaches to save the day? Surely they were not going to allow the Singapore Naval Base to fall into Jap hands. It was a vital stronghold in the Far East. We little realised that we had already been left for dead. Our wild hopes continued, however, as is often the case with desperate men and we clung to every rumour that came our way. But now Nippon ruled the majority of Burma, Thailand, Malaya and a large part of Singapore, the sea and skies alike. The Yanks were close, rumour had it. A million optimistic ideas and thoughts had held sway, long enough to give us the strength to load another gun, fire another shot. Now all those hopes were fading fast. The fiery, blasting, bloody living hell that Singapore had become now told its own cynical truth.

Every artillery piece that could fire had been dragged to the beach, almost at water's edge, and with piles of ammo and charge cases around them, sang their last staccato song. Great palls of smoke hung over the City and beach. Jap planes screamed overhead and swooped low over the guns shooting up all and sundry. Miles of burnt out cars and trucks lined the beach road – and the men who still held on to sanity did what was required of them.

On the 22nd February, 1942 Singapore, City of the Lion, was ceremoniously handed over to the successful Japanese Invader. Many times has the question been argued, could we have held out longer? Was it a walkover for the Jap? Why this, why that! Only those in top authority know the real answer, we, the mere pawns in the great game of war, knew but little. But certain facts remain. By holding out as long as we did, 12 weeks or thereabouts, the Japs calculated attack on Australia was delayed long enough to allow the Allies to be ready for him. There is little doubt that had we succumbed as easily as Jap calculated, nothing would have stopped him flooding into Australia – and he would have been there for the duration had that happened – pinning down many thousands of Allied forces. Such was his intention. The boys of Singapore stopped him from doing just that.

I have always thought it strange that the Malayan Campaign has been looked upon by many official sources as a dirty word in the military annals. That such sacrifice and heroism can be decorated with such an insult beggars description. We were a half trained, half equipped, Fred Karno's army. Unblooded and inexperienced in jungle warfare. Pitted against a superb jungle trained fighting man, powerfully armed, with full air support – is it small wonder that events turned out as they did? To have continued further with the resistance on the Island would, I feel sure, only have resulted in wholesale slaughter of the defenders and also the civilian population who, for the most part, were innocent participants in the event. It is remarkable however, that offers by the Chinese Communist Guerilla Army to throw in their lot with us were refused by our own Command. These trained jungle fighters promptly faded into the surrounding islands and a valuable ally was lost. Was this another example of British Army Red Tape? I wonder!

With the last shot fired, the last need for maximum effort gone and the silent cannon around us, a hush akin to the grave descended. I began to feel uplifted and downcast all at once. Now it was over, but what happened next? Many tales had been told of the Japanese atrocities in China and even up country during the Campaign. Was it just propaganda? Everywhere Jap circulars told us 'if we were good soldiers we would be well treated by our Jap Masters'. I think we actually believed them, because we wanted to. 'There will be working parties wanted to clear up the mess', we were told. But afterwards? Well – Japan belonged to the Geneva Convention, he would treat us alright – we hoped! Nothing to do but laze in the sun. It was then that I got my first urge to start drawing seriously again. During the Campaign I had done several sketches of various actions, guns, planes, men fighting etc., but now I thought I would do a complete set of pictures of everything I had seen and was yet to see. Gifted with a photographic memory this was easy for me. I set to work with bits of paper found lying around and what remained of my water colours. We were soon marched out to a prepared P.O.W. camp at Changi Jail. Being allowed to take all we could carry, we set off under guard; prams, suitcases, anything was used to carry our precious belongings to our new home. All I had was a shoulder pack containing a blanket, mess tin etc., a change of clothes and three pieces of valuable drawing paper. An old box of paints I had found on a dump provided my nucleus for the work I had set myself.

As we marched through the now shattered and stinking streets of the city on our way to Changi, shouts of derision and scorn met our ears. The locals, mainly Tamils, sneered openly and screamed abuse and filth at us. Little aware of their own fate awaiting them at the hands of their new masters, they were eager to display their pro Japanese feelings in the hope that they would find favour in the days ahead with the new occupying troops of Imperial Japan.

But the average Britisher is unshaken by the howls of jackals and we turned but few heads to listen to the mob. Everywhere drains and ditches were filled with corpses and decaying bodies. Dead Sikhs lay half in and half out of army trucks; congealed blood lay in great pools across the pavements, attracting flies in great numbers and turning our stomachs over as we passed by.

Once clear of the City, the clean, fresh sea air filled our lungs and we began to hold up our heads a little. By midday with the sun full overhead, the effects of the last week began to catch up with us. A few of us who had begun a marching song dried up and only the trudging of tired, dusty feet was heard.

Suddenly a column of women with children in their arms approached us from the opposite direction. Some were relatives and wives of the men in our own column. Emotions began to run high and the Jap guards, suspecting trouble, rattled their rifle bolts and exploded into staccato orders to walk faster. The women straightened their shoulders and began to sing 'There'll always be an England'. That did it! Tears flooded our eyes but we were in control again. The song became a roar that even the Jap could not compete with and, as the two columns passed each other, we knew that somehow we could – and would – stick it out to the bitter end.

▲ 1st Japanese landing — Kota Bahru, North East Malaya

▼ Endau — Japanese Zero's mass attack on obsolete
      British Aircraft

▲ Australian troops hemmed in by Japanese pincer attack North Malaya

▼ Slim River — Kedah — Malaya — Decisive battle with Japanese tanks which finally broke the British line

▲ Loyal Chinese villagers help and feed cut off British survivors lost in jungle

▼ Gunners bayonet charge to save gun in rubber tree plantation

▲ Signallers laying telephone line through swamp in tropical storm

▲ Various Indian troops retreat through heavy jungle

▲ Bombed Red Cross first aid post on main road to Singapore

▲ Bombing of British reinforcements arriving in Straits of Singapore

▼ Bombing of Singapore by Japanese bombers

▲ Burning oil from shelled dumps floats down Singapore river

▼ Theatre converted into First Aid Station on sea front, Singapore — last week of fighting

▲ Japanese attempt to cross repaired causeway, caught by British shell fire

▼ Singapores last stand — remnants of artillery fire constant barrage under heavy air attacks

▲ British and Australian High Command surrender to Japanese

▼ After capitulation Allied troops now P.O.W's begin long march to prison camps outside Singapore

CHAPTER 5

THE BEGINNING OF THE LONG WAIT
– THE TREK UP COUNTRY

Our quarters at Changi, in what was called Birdwood Camp, were once British Army billets, good, dry huts. For some weeks, apart from working parties around the area, cleaning up the aftermath of war, burying dead bodies (such as hundreds of Chinese civilians who had been tied together with barbed wire and then shot and left on the beach to rot), we were allowed to take things pretty easy. If this is the worst we can expect, we told ourselves, we can stick it out for the duration. The climate was wonderful. Sunshine all day long.

Gradually we began to relax from the ordeal of the fall of Singapore and all it had meant to us. But, as always, there was a snag. Because of our great numbers something like 80,000 P.O.W.'s were now in Jap hands on the Island, and our own Officers were still in charge but answerable to the Japs for our behaviour. The order of the day was this; O.R.'s were paid a few cents per week, if they worked. If sick and unable to work – no pay. This was a Jap order. Officers received about half their normal army pay whether they worked or not. Many did work and pulled their weight but some didn't! Spending their time playing cards, smoking Chinese cigars, brewing coffee and lounging around the camp, generally making life disagreeable for all lower ranks. My own C.O., Major W. E. Gill, was a splendid example of what an Officer should be. Organising a sick pay fund, he asked Officers to contribute each week towards getting extra food for the sick. This could be bought from local traders occasionally. About this time we were put on a greatly reduced diet. Until then we had been living fairly well on Army food but now it became one third European food, two thirds Asiatic food.

This great reduction in our diet soon made itself felt in a hundred ways. Saying that European food supplies were already gone (a fact we soon discovered was quite untrue) the Jap brought in supplies of low quality rice, poor vegetables and a fresh meat issue each week – which amounted to one piece per man the size of a sugar cube, floating in half a pint of greasy water called stew. Heated arguments broke out between men struggling to obtain sufficient food for their needs, many often accusing cooks and Messing Officers of unfair allocation of rations. When a man's stomach is empty his reason becomes unbalanced and greed holds sway. Already the rat race was starting. Of the M.O.'s at this time I speak highly on the whole, a few couldn't care less, but most did their best for all. Dysentery and beri-beri, skin sores and general debility were now rife everywhere. I went down with dysentery and dropped to eight stone from twelve stone eight pounds. Taken to camp hospital, I was put on a diet of rice water and peanuts. Many men died from this treatment as much as the diseases, being unable to consume the nauseating mixture. At this time ample food supplies were held in reserve by our own Officers and it could have been issued to the sick, but it wasn't. The excuse was that 'we must save it in case the Japs reduced our diet still further'. What did happen was that the Jap, on inspection of the camps, decided that if we could afford to save food we were getting too much, and did reduce the issue at once – even for hospitals. So much for the misguided and muddled thinking of some of those in command.

About this time, May 1942, the Japanese issued a printed form demanding that all men sign it. The terms read to the effect that we promised not to try to escape on penalty of death. All ranks refused to sign and the entire P.O.W. population of Changi were herded together in Selerang Barracks, a large but nowhere near large enough area. Thousands of men were crammed into this compound for four days. Sleeping space was one square foot per two men. So resting in relays was necessary in order to sleep at all. Latrine pits were dug in the Parade Ground and men queued for hours to use them. Flies thronged by the millions, disease broke out in profusion – but we did not sign. Eventually we were returned to our own areas, confident of our victory over the Jap. Life now continued as before but an under-current of suspicion was creeping into our minds. Had we really beaten the Jap in a mental trial of strength or had he something else in store? We had not very long to wait to find out. A few weeks later our Officers were told by the Jap that wonderful new rest camps had been built for the sick P.O.W.'s in Thailand. All men were invited to volunteer for these camps. The lucky ones would leave in five days time. I was one of the lucky ones. The time of departure came and we were loaded into trucks, taken to the station and herded onto the trains like cattle. Steel ammunition trucks were our Hospital Trains. Heat traps at the best of times. Into these between 30 and 50 men were pushed, and off we went.

Once again I was lucky. Our truck held the left overs, only 26 men shared the metal oven. Nearly all were sick men and I was still suffering from dysentery. This trifling complaint sometimes necessitates attending the latrines up to 50 times daily and there were ten others like me in the same truck. One bucket was provided for this function, one bucket for food – and that was it! Food was distributed from an army dixie filled with boiled rice, and in the appalling heat this very soon went sour. For five days these luxurious conditions prevailed. Some men died and were buried en route without Military Honours I fear and many of us wished we were dead too. From soaring hopes to this, in a matter of hours. Now we knew, or did we? Perhaps this was all the transport Jap had to take us to our rest camps. No actual brutal acts happened on the journey that I heard of. So we gave Nip the benefit of the doubt. I occupied my time by making small sketches, as is shown here, on an old notepad I had found and a piece of charcoal. The stink of bodies, the everlasting hum of flies, the rattle of the train, lulled me to sleep too often but I forced myself to stay awake long enough to record a number of these situations. In spite of the dejection around me I was feeling a strange exultation. At last my life as an artist was beginning to mean something to me. Here was my chance to be the war artist I had always wanted to be. The price did not seem too much. I had a job to do and I meant to do it as long as I could still breathe.

As the journey dragged on, though no actual beatings took place, the Jap's attitude towards us was changing. Always sullen, he became more so, shouting obscenities in Japanese, holding us up for derision to the local natives in villages we passed through and generally rubbing it in that we were slaves of Nippon. Few of us had any money but we were desperate for food, good food, and parched by the heat many of us traded personal treasures such as watches given to us by loved ones in return for a drink of water or a bottle of cheap native wine. A bunch of bananas was only traded by a grinning native for a high price such as a pair of trousers or a spare shirt. Many of us that day began to learn the gentle art of thieving. Clean minded, decent lads suddenly became petty crooks in an attempt to keep body and soul together. I covered a farthing with silver paper and got one small loaf in return but only just before the infuriated native discovered the deception. Yelling abuse, he tried to climb on the train to take the matter further but fortunately for me the train began to move and he departed in wrath. When I finally opened the bread roll I found it was mouldy inside, not even worth the farthing I gave for it – but I still enjoyed the taste of bread again, such as it was.

As the journey by train continued, presumably towards our wonderful new rest camp, speculation grew as to what they would be like and where they would be located. We found it hard to imagine how any such camp existed, especially as the war had been over so quickly. However, it was assumed by some that the camps were probably on the fringe of some big town and in any event would be run by International Red Cross – or at least supervised by them. And so the matter rested there. By now the rate of sickness had increased enormously in the shape of many severe cases of dysentery. This unholy scourge was at all times our worst enemy, apart from the Jap himself, that is. Although orders were that to leave the train without permission could bring a rifle shot in our direction, the urge and physical necessity of dysentery sufferers would blind them to such an extent as to leap out of the trucks whenever they stopped for some reason or another, often emitting a trail of blood in the process. No washing facilities at all being available, the condition of our clothes leaves little to the imagination. A brief sojourn in the adjoining ditches and then back to the train as it moved off. An ideal opportunity to escape you may say, but to where and with what? No knowledge of the language, sick or ill, hungry, ill clothed and the constant prey of treacherous local natives who would sell you for a packet of cigarettes – we had no chance. An odd few men did have a go and were never heard of again.

Eventually, one magnificent golden tropical dawn, our cavalcade of steel trucks rumbled to a creaking, grinding halt at our destination. Known as Ban Pong it consisted of a main street flanked by Indian shops and huts and Chinese street stalls intermingled here and there. Bleary eyed and stiff, we dragged ourselves out of the trucks, gathered up our few belongings, and with grunting Nips around us, trudged inland. Those in charge of us directed us to the market square where we were to be given a meal. Although only a matter of half a mile or so, many men could hardly walk at all. Sloe eyed Thai children ran excitedly forward, offering to carry our sparse luggage. Some of them promptly disappeared down a nearby alley, taking a load of kit with them. Few men had sufficient energy to chase them. Some informed the Nip guards and promptly received a blow from a rifle butt for their pains. Of such was the kingdom of Nip! To me, though very tired, the sky had great fascination. Dark, weird shaped clouds were slowly creeping across a brilliant yellow sky. One cloud in particular impressed and depressed me immensely. It had the shape of a great demon with outstretched, clawlike hand, as if to engulf us all. If such omens can be taken seriously, then here was a forecast of great evil to come. Our first meal consisted of a pint of boiled rice, no seasoning, one pint of stew – green leaves and a kind of marrow chopped up and floating on the surface – and a pint of tea – no milk or sugar. To us it tasted great and some men even got a second helping.

We were allowed to rest until the evening of that day, even allowed a brief wash at the local village pump. Then a long, long sleep in the shade of a hut or tree. Not allowed to wander about or talk to natives, we hardly appreciated the magnificent colours of the villagers' saris or the wares and foods on sale everywhere. Food was in profusion. With money we could have lived well, or the Jap could have issued it to us but he did not. Again the question arose, where are the rest camps? A Warrant Officer of our party approached a Jap Officer, saluted him – as was the order of the day – and asked politely where our rest camps were. The Jap burst into loud laughter. 'No rest camp for British pig' he yelled. 'All men work, and work, and work – for all long time'. The W.O. tried to explain, thinking the Jap mistook us for a working party; 'But Nippon, we are all sick men, some of us cannot even walk.' 'Then those who cannot walk will die!' snapped the Jap. Tapping his pistol holster significantly – and warming to his theme – he bellowed, 'No men sick from now on. All men fit. All men work for great Nippon Emperor.' Then, seeing a tattoo of a crucifix on a P.O.W.'s chest he went up to the man, punched him in the ribs and said 'Tojo Number One now, not Jesus Christ – him finished!' With this stunning revelation our hopes hit zero. None of us spoke for some time and that evening we began the first leg of the nightmarish march to what was to be one of the base camps for the Railway of Death.

Now that we knew at last the truth, a truth that had been at the back of our minds for some time, the whole aspect of our life changed. Everything Jap had said was a lie – rest camps for the sick etc. Sheer utter bunk! It was just another form of Japanese humour, we decided. To have told us straight out in Singapore that the sick men were to be used as slave labour could have incited another trial of strength between our Officers and the Jap so he had used a different method to get us up country, and it had worked. Knowing that the initial jungle clearing for the Railway would be the toughest work, he hoped to kill off all sick men first. Hard to believe but that was Jap's way of doing things.

We marched all through the night, with only a few minutes rest every hour. Along mud covered roads and paths, at times hardly able to see far in front of us. But any lagging soon produced a dig from a bayonet point and a growl from the guards of 'Speedo'. Dawn was breaking as we finally got the order to stop and rest for an hour. We dropped where we were, in the mud, and slept like dead men. Someone lit a fire to make a hot drink of tea, but many men were already asleep. I stayed awake just long enough to mentally photograph the scene, to draw in full later, then I too slept.

The following day we spent in making a rough camp site. There were no huts, just a few old army tents. It rained all day but we toiled to make rough shelters out of palm fronds and branches, after which a meal of the usual rice slush came up. And so to bed. I awoke several times during the night with violent stomach pains and dragged myself to a nearby ditch. Once there I had to remain for about twenty minutes, fighting the demands of nature with a desire for sleep and a slightly drier domain. My tent, a groundsheet on branches, was inches deep in water by now but I finally returned feeling deadly weak, crying to myself one minute and despising myself the next for so doing. 'You are a weak fool' I told myself. 'To do the job you have set yourself you have got to be a lot tougher than this, so belt up!' I can't remember who really won the argument, I was asleep by this time, face down in the mud a couple of feet away from my tent. I awoke next morning feeling stronger – how, I haven't a clue. Probably the spirit force that I felt guided me had taken over. In all events I recovered enough to work along with my comrades on the job of clearing the jungle in our vicinity and with the coming of evening had made my tent more weatherproof. That night I slept well.

We stayed only a few days at this camp. I never knew its actual name, if it had one. Then we moved on bound for Tonchon South, a Base camp that was to feed supplies to other working parties in the area. The march there was tougher than our first from Ban Pong. The road as such was non existent consisting only of deep tracks, waterlogged and slimy. We clawed, slipped and cursed our way up the mountain side in weather varying from torrential rain to scorching heat. By now several men had died. We had no Padre with us so their funerals were scanty affairs, scanty in every way as they were buried almost naked. Their clothes and belongings had disappeared overnight. Already there were those of us with the carrion instinct well developed. No sooner had a man given up his ghost than his sacred possessions – a photograph of a wife, a child, any money, blanket and bowl and spoon etc. – just went. The law of the jungle transmits itself very rapidly to those who venture its paths of terror. You could not blame such pilfering under these circumstances. Such objects could provide food to live at some later occasion. They were objects to be used for barter with the natives. To know all is to understand all. I was fast beginning to understand the complexity and the frailty of human nature. The real blame lay in our slave masters who could have prevented such acts by a little humane treatment to those who now lay under their heels.

CHAPTER 6

THE RAILWAY CAMPS

During the short space of time in Singapore men had already begun a long series of mental battles with themselves. Some had lost the first round but had survived to fight again. Others had given up for good and were already dead, one way or another. To live is to be in command of oneself – at all times. Beyond that is certain death and as each weary day dragged on you either learnt that mastery or you fell by the wayside. I do in no way decry religion of any sort, but it was proved countless times that to accept everything as the will of God led only to despair and defeat. Many friends of mine died from complaints that were not fatal, but they believed so little in their own will power that they just gave in before they were really beaten. Others dogmatically and persistently held on to life – fighting the most agonising pain and disease – and lived. I found religion as such a very inadequate power to combat conditions such as we were now encountering.

Very few Padres I met proved to be staunch believers in their own preaching. Padre Duckworth, whom I knew, was an exception of distinction. If ever a man of God walked that vicious land, helping, healing and inspiring all he met, that man was he. He was much loved by all.

The heavy rail laying of the Railway had not yet begun but working parties were busy every day, from 12 to 16 hours, breaking boulders, tree felling and ramp building. At this time I had again contracted dysentery, a bad case. I was lucky to be allowed to do a light job. Fetching food supplies from barges on the river, we tramped three miles there and three back with heavy loads of vegetables, many unfit for human consumption, but still edible for P.O.W.'s. During brief rests on such jobs I managed to knock out a few rough sketches of conditions around us. On one such occasion a Jap guard saw me drawing. He came over and I waited for the blow to fall. Instead he pulled out a snap of his family, all twelve of them, himself in the middle in full ceremonial uniform. 'You draw' he commanded, 'Come.' He led me to his tent. He was a Gunson, (Sgt. Major) and lived in luxury. I was given a sheet of notepaper and I set to work – smelling good Jap food around me I purposely dragged the job out to last the day. When it was finished he glared at it, made me alter the oriental eyes to a western shape, and then gave me an enormous omelette to eat. Such good food and so much was beyond my stomach. I ate half and took the remainder back to my pals in camp – they fell on it ravenously.

The next few weeks were a combination of monotony, fiendishly exhausting work and a deadly nausea. The Railway we now learned was to be built from Ban Pong to Mulmein. Its purpose was to carry Jap troops to and from Singapore and also give Nip a line of supply for the Burma fighting now in progress. This titanic job had been attempted in peace time by civilian contractors but given up before it left the planning stage on paper as being utterly impossible and impracticable. At the command of the Son of Heaven, Hirohito, and his arch villains the job was now not only possible but had to be expedited – if necessary over the bodies of P.O.W.'s. This was personally read out to us by Jap Officers. No stone or skull was to be left unturned in order to achieve this object. Jap guards and Engineers had total authority over all Allied Officers and men – and they took a personal delight in carrying out these instructions. No form of cruelty or devilry was too base for them to perpetrate on our skinny frames. And furthermore, to humiliate and debase us was to them an achievement. The Japanese themselves have repudiated these facts many times but in their hearts they know it to be true. If a good generation is to rise from those bitter days I will be the first to be glad of it. I no longer bear a personal grudge to my former captors. I do not doubt that fate itself has already dealt with them. Every age has had its barbarians, let us hope that Japan's has now passed. The example set by Nippon in Thailand was readily adopted by many local natives who often demanded payment for drinking water and other camp facilities normally free.

Food, never plentiful, was now hit by the Monsoon Season. During this period both Thailand and Burma become a sea of water and mud. Rivers flooded and barges carrying food up stream to us were often lost, the occupants drowned and the precious food, such as it was, destroyed. Many friends of mine were killed in this manner. Chaos upon chaos was often the order of the day and to survive the continuous chain of ordeals one had to mentally detach oneself completely from one's surroundings. The food issue in some of the worst hit camps was two meals only per day, consisting of three-quarters of a pint of evil smelling rice, the usual vegetable stew and quite often that was it. No water or tea to drink. A Jap Officer we nicknamed 'Little Hitler' would supervise the dealing out of each meal and woe betide any over-generous cook or mess orderly who gave a few grains of rice too much to a friend who was more ill than the rest. He would receive a 'bashing' on the spot. Men were desperate for food and many would hang around the Japs' tent during meal times, begging for the scraps. The Nips would keep them waiting a long time and finally would put down one mess tin containing a few left overs, motion the men to stand in a circle until they gave the word 'go'. The P.O.W.'s would then literally fight amongst themselves for what remained. I could not blame them, but neither could I bring myself to join them. The ever present fear of dysentery and cholera warned me of such folly.

By now the diet we were forced to accept as our daily sustenance, a diet so totally deficient in essential vitamin and calorie content, was taking a full toll of our bodies. With the total absence of strength giving qualities in our food, each man was down to the level of living off the marrow in his own bones, so to speak. This was the opinion of many of our Medical Officers. With no hope of the food being greatly improved until the cessation of hostilities the outlook was indeed frightening to say the least. These facts, added to the terribly hard work expected of us, rapidly took a heavy toll on men's lives. Almost every kind of complaint or disease was rife and men working absurdly long hours in the jungle clearings and on the Railway dropped and died where they worked. Even light duty men, those suffering from jungle ulcers on legs and arms, severe skin complaints and dysentery were forced to carry heavy logs long distances. Four men would be needed to lift a log about ten feet long by one foot in diameter – exactly the same item that an elephant could lift with its trunk. I lived in a camp like this and so I can absolutely vouch for the truth of these statements. It was the same in all of the eight jungle camps I was in.

Now the dreaded 'Speedo' campaign was at its height. Total pressure of work by all men was demanded. Direct from Tokio came this order and the penalties were increased on those too weak to work or anyone trying to evade this inhuman degree of labour. A day and night shift was now used in all camps in Burma and Thailand. To make up working parties to full strength, barely returned from a long, sweating day under a tropical sun, on pig swill diet, beaten, tortured even, we were hounded out of our stinking huts and shelters to trek back along the mud and slime that led to the Railway cutting. A lashing in store for any sick soul who faltered on the way and possibly a bayonet or bullet.

The working parties were often full of desperately ill men, suffering from malaria and dysentery, breaking heavy rocks that lay in the path of the advancing rail tracks. Under the watchful eye of the Korean Guard they worked until told to stop, under penalty of death.

And as we P.O.W.'s toiled unceasingly, unknown to us the war in Burma was going badly for the Japanese. With the Railway still incomplete, and this in spite of titanic efforts by slave labour, his troops were forced to march a great deal of the way to the front. The heavy Monsoon was now upon us and the so-called roads were a sea of deep mud that sucked and dragged at the feet like an octopus. Watching the Nip Infantry trail past our camp each day we could almost feel sorry for them. Their poor beasts of burden, mules and yaks squealed their protests at every step. This was jungle warfare with the boot on the other foot. This time the Jap was having a rough journey instead. Heavy, clinging mist hung in the trees and air above, reminding one of the Island of Monsters or a lost world, as indeed we felt we were in at times. To this day I cannot remember how I managed to keep drawing and painting but somehow I did. Often half asleep, returning from a working party, I would gulp down my food and, hiding in a dark corner of a hut or tent, scribble away at a situation I had seen during the day. I had now developed a nasty ulcer on my left foot that smelt like gangrene. No clean dressings being available I wrapped a puttee around it and hoped for the best.

I shared a tent at this time with six other men, the size of it being about six foot by four so the amount of space per man speaks for itself. One of them, Jimmy Faulkes, a sickbay orderly, managed to get me a tin oil lamp. After lights out he would hold the lamp for me to draw by. He was devoted and kind to me in many ways. I was blessed with many such good friends and without their help would never have achieved these pictures. I owe them much. My paints I now had to devise out of anything that came to hand. Clay mixed with water and grease, juice from roots and even flower stems. Dutch troops with us told me how to do this for which I am eternally grateful.

One man in our tent, Jock we will call him, from Glasgow, could never do enough for me. He brought me water when I was ill and even stole food for me, from where he would never say – so as not to incriminate me I think. He died just before I left that camp and I recorded in a drawing the look on his face the week prior to his death. He never complained unnecessarily but to me he typified us all. I called his picture 'King of the Damned' – for such we were.

We had now been marched further up the line to cut a channel for the track to pass through. We made camp on a small plateau. Ringed by high mountains smothered in mist it seemed like the top of the world indeed. Our journey there had been through dense bamboo jungle. Cutting our way a yard at a time with pangas our legs and arms were torn and scratched frequently by murderous bamboo thorns that protruded everywhere. Here and there along the tracks already cut by other parties we found the skeletons of former comrades, littering the deep grass like the bones of animals. Sometimes they were covered by giant 'Bull Ants' – red and black and of great size. Marching in thousands upon thousands these fearsome creatures eat all in their path. Only fire will stop them. Many times they invaded our camps, often attacking the living as well as the dead. I do believe that had they been edible we would have eaten them. As it was we caught and ate many strange rodents and snakes, Iguana and birds. The jungle snail is quite big and quite tasty, to one who is starving that is. What food there was in camp was now doled out sparingly by the Nips who were also feeling the pinch.

The camp we were in had no sick bay at all and men who fell sick stayed in their hut built of green bamboo. Stayed in their hut if allowed by Nip to do so, that is. More often than not he would kick you out to work and die. But even the Jap sometimes could not stomach the appalling sights that took the eye in these foul holes we called camps. The stench of our bodies alone was one thing, but add to that the dysentery cases, unable to move, no one to care for them, unable to crawl to the pit that served as a latrine. They lay and suffered in their utter misery – some too far gone towards death to know their friends. Many were stark naked and filthy, no washing water was allowed. They presented us with an added depression as we returned from work at night, to eat and sleep alongside them. Many times have I thought to myself in those long nights – 'there but for the grace of God go I'. Indeed, I did a sketch of such a hut under the same conditions and for me to look again upon it brings back all the stench and horrors that were once my life.

Quite often these days it is common to watch T.V. programmes of animal and bird life in various parts of the world. Creatures, reptiles and even vultures are extolled for various virtues they are supposed to possess. But to me the vulture is to this day an omen of death and all that is vile. These revolting birds cast a hideous shadow on our lives as P.O.W.'s in Burma and Thailand. For hours and hours they would sit in the trees around us, waiting – always waiting for one of us to die. And when a man did drop dead, through exhaustion or cruelty, the carrion kings of the sky would set up a series of screeching cries to one another, telling their brood of more meat for the having – that is, if the man was left were he fell, as many were. Often the Nip would allow no man to go to the help of a fallen comrade or even bury the dead decently and when this happened the vultures would descend in high glee to do justice to a good meal. But these foul birds, evil looking and evil smelling as they were, did not always do the eating. I have one true story on record of a vulture, too full to fly after a heavy gorging session, being set upon by ravenous P.O.W.'s, killed and cooked like a turkey. Some of them died as a result, but this macabre episode explains vividly the terrible state of mind that the Death Railway caused men to be in on certain occasions.

CHAPTER 7

BRIDGE BUILDING, THE 'RIVER KWAI'

Hundreds of men had now been moved still further up country into the 'Valley of the Kwai' to build the notorious bridge there. Though not actually working on the bridge myself I was very close to the scene of operations and saw a great deal of what went on as regards the construction of the bridge and the men that built it. There were other bridges of less importance that spanned various rivers and ravines and the Jap treatment of P.O.W.'s was similar everywhere. Men worked eight hour shifts, sometimes marching three or four miles to and from the building site twice daily. Along roads a foot deep in thick, black mud with torrential rain beating down. Many men died on the road and were left to rot. It is impossible to convey our true feelings at this time, so utterly degraded and debased had we become. Low grade human animals that had once been cheerful, lighthearted youths such as one sees on the streets of today or lounging in the Coffee Bars with their sexy girl friends. We had had such dreams of a gay, youthful manhood but ours was to be spent in the Hell Camps of the Jap overlord – and like the galley slaves of distant time, only under worse conditions, we many times prayed for death.

Whatever the devilry of the Jap, he was brilliant in the art of 'make do'. Realising that army trucks were useless on the mud soaked roads, he calmly removed the wheels and ran the trucks on the rails of the tracks. Being the same gauge was either accidental or planned, I never knew which. It is sufficient to say that the idea worked very well and the Nip saved precious engine fuel that way too. P.O.W.'s, Indians, Chinese coolies, Malays and Thais were loaded on that 'train' and trundled up country by their thousands – every vestige of room being used. Most bridges were made of tree trunks, tier upon tier, piled high and slotted together or tied native fashion. The genius of the Jap engineers did them credit. This mountainous country is awesome enough in itself, but travelling thus in our condition over bridges that creaked and groaned was akin to a nightmare, particularly as many of our boys, anxious to sabotage the Jap war effort, had often inserted white ants into the foundations of the bridge supports. The ants must have been pro Jap as I never heard of a bridge collapsing!

Looking back it is still an amazing fact, even to me, that any man survived at all. Had we been fit men to start with the hazards in themselves would have been sufficient to kill an average man. But added to this was the ever present disease and filth that beggars description. Cholera was now making its presence felt in many camps and stories came through of literally hundreds of men dying in one camp almost overnight. It is certainly true to say that many men, suffering such diseases, were driven out to work in raging rivers to make and repair bridges in all weathers. Underfed and beside themselves with pain and misery these heroes carried on until they dropped. These men did not die gloriously under a military standard maybe – but no soldier in uniform or out of it, on any field of conflict, ever carried himself with greater personal bravery than did the men of the Hell Camps. Even the rats amongst us, and rats there were, can be forgiven their petty crimes. We had now reached the state where to live and survive every man must put himself first. Those that did not greatly reduced their chances of survival. There have been very few films made of the war out East, never one of the Malayan Campaign, this black spot in British history, and those that have been made bear only a slight resemblance to the actual conditions. Most of the public who have seen them have therefore, either got the impression that they have been exaggerated, glamorised or just simply not true. The Press have usually labelled them as horror films and played them down or else given them publicity because of the outstanding star taking the leading role. Mentally we were too tired for heroic deeds and in nine cases out of ten morale in camps was pathetically low. Many of the Officers who had remained behind in Singapore and even those sick men who had never come up country found it hard to believe the truth when it was finally told to them. There are still to this day the odd handful of ex P.O.W.'s of various ranks who did indeed have a cushy time of it. Nothing, not even whistling or singing a patriotic song, could have lifted us out of the zombie like existence to which we had degenerated. Every ounce of breath and energy was needed to stay alive.

But though selfishness was now the order of the day amongst many P.O.W.'s, there were still those who clung to their beliefs; Christianity, Catholicism or whatever they happened to accept. I had always been something of a Spiritualist. I say 'something' because I actually knew very little of this deep science. I had, however, had many wonderful experiences, happenings which others had witnessed and could not deny. With the advance of starvation conditions I found my sensitivity towards these things more acute and even though I was sorely tempted to allow myself to degenerate mentally as other poor souls had done, I was always pulled away from the actual deed just in time. Sometimes despising myself for being cowardly. Many times I could have gone the absolute maximum in greed and cruelty but in my weakest moment managed to master the emotion. It was in the darkest days of 'Speedo' when we lived in a dream, by day and night, awoke at dawn, ate our tin of slops in pouring rain and set out for yet another day of jungle hell, that I really became fully aware of the spiritual power that was taking over within me. That same power took me right through those awful days and is with me yet for which I'm not ashamed to give my thanks. May it never leave me.

The average physical condition and mental dejection of most men who dragged their weary feet mile after mile up and down the jungle tracks and roads was extremely poor. Two men were usually detailed each day to look after the food whilst out on the working party. Carrying our own tools, 'chunkels' as they were called, the Asiatic equivalent of a spade, a tin of rice mixed, if we were lucky, with vegetables and a small bag of tea. On arriving at the work site they would build a fire and brew up. Brewing up could take anything from half an hour to two hours, depending on the mood of the Nip guard in charge. If he had spent a good night with a local Thai girl the evening before and was in good spirits, he might even go so far as to allow us to have a drink of tea right away and even hand out the odd cigarette or two. Most times though he would sullenly watch us for the slightest misdemeanour such as taking a brief rest when not ordered to do so – and land out left and right with his bamboo cane. Many times I have personally fallen foul of the antics of our little friends when I particularly wanted to memorise a situation that I needed for a drawing to be done later.

▲ Five day train journey to Thailand by P.O.W. to start building railway for Japanese — men relieving themselves in ditches. No sanitation on trains.

▼ P.O.W. Begin march through Thailand in monsoon conditions. Many men sick and dying

▲ Primary construction of bridge in Kwai Valley

▲ Burning of Cholera dead on bamboo fires in jungle

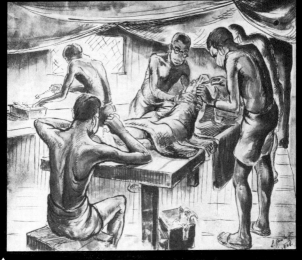

▲ Amputation of man's leg by primitive instruments
Tamakhan Bridge camp

▼ Artist — Author has tooth removed by Australian dentist
in jungle hospital camp

▲ Cholera isolation tent full of dying men

▼ Wampo — Bridge — Viaduct — built around cliff face by P.O.W. labour

Tambaji (BURMA).

GOVERNMENT HOUSE SINGAPORE

(sectional view) of river.

FISH CLEANING, SCABIES & SORES: IN JUNGLE STREAM

▲ Man lying in river to let tiny fish eat Bacteria from ulcers on body

▼ Dysentery cases using primitive latrine in jungle

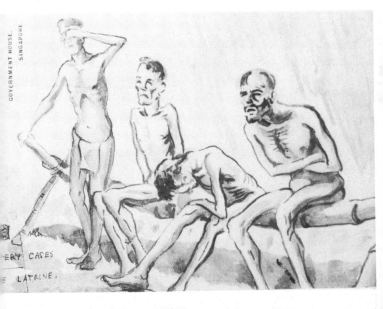

GOVERNMENT HOUSE. SINGAPORE

...ERY CASES

...= LATRINE.

▲ Hut full of dying Tamils and Allied P.O.W.

▼ Singapore hospital ward – medical orderlies scraping ulcers with spoons to clean wounds. No anasthetic used

GOVERNMENT HOUSE, SINGAPORE.

KHANBURI HOSPITAL CAMP. 1943.

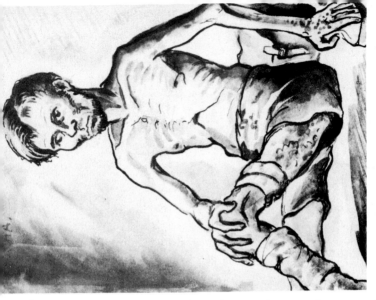

▲ Average condition of most men returning from jungle

▼ Skin diseases suffered by men returning from work on railway in Thailand

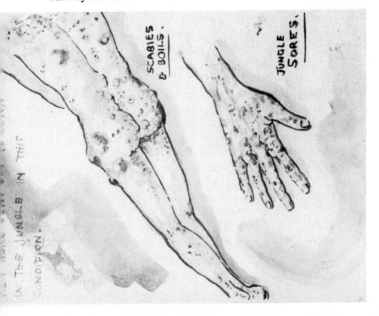

▲ Public beating of P.O.W. by Japanese guards for hitting guard in self defence — Changi

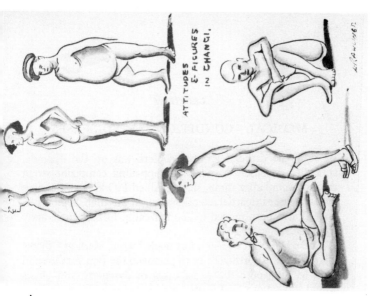

▲ General effects of mainly rice diet on men in most camps

▼ British, Australian and Javanese supplementing diet with snails, home made food from jungle fruits when available — and making hospital bed pans from bamboo

CHAPTER 8

MEDICAL – CONDITIONS AND DISEASES

By now the dreaded scourge cholera was on the upgrade, spreading at fantastic speed this appalling complaint swept through camp after camp, slaying Allied P.O.W.'s and natives with the same impartial relentlessness. At this time, September, 1944, I had been moved to another camp further back, away from the Railway.

There had been a great effort made by our Medical Officers who had come north with us to persuade the Japs that to send back to Singapore the worst cases of dysentery and ulcers would leave more food for the working parties. Various other reasons were given and at last (probably somewhat influenced by Anthony Eden's (now Lord Avon) warning that the Japs would be taken to task for any barbaric practices on P.O.W.'s) agreed to do this. I was one of the fortunate ones selected to return and I mentally gave thanks. We were taken by trucks to that part of the Railway that was now in operation and were duly despatched to a transit camp – the name of which I forget. It was teeming with dying natives, all in the throes of dysentery and cholera. Coloured and white slept together in the same huts. Clad in rags or even naked, we huddled together during the cold, wet nights. Natives and P.O.W.'s alike, unable to control themselves, emitted vomit and excreta everywhere.

Each day a number of P.O.W.'s who could still walk were detailed to carry out those men and natives who had died during the night. The stench of death was everywhere, an almost sweet, sickly smell that defied description. We had long since passed the stage of trying to protect ourselves against contamination from the dead or dying. If we got it, we got it and that was that! Many times I wondered why I was still alive and though visiting the latrine myself some forty times daily, was somehow still able to believe myself untouched by all around me. For me to claim that I was protected beyond all others would be impertinent and conceited, not to say unjust to all those other fine men who died in agony. But at times it certainly seemed as if this must be so. For what purpose at that time I could not imagine unless it be that someone had to survive who could record the abominable conditions that man can live under and why so many boys died. I vowed to myself that if this was so, then I would not rest until as many people in the world as possible had been told the truth – and I would dedicate myself to that end, always.

As the rapidly mounting dead were taken from the huts and ditches where they had died, out to the nearby jungle, great fires were lit to cremate their withered remains as quickly as possible. To bury cholera dead only multiplies the disease as the germ is eventually washed through the earth by rain to lower ground levels and eventually rivers and is carried downstream to give birth to another outbreak at some distant time. We were now experts in cholera and all that it meant. Being water borne or rising in a mist from the ground, according to the country and conditions, it is carried on its deadly journey by insects and flies. Flies thronged our camps in the millions. Our latrine pits soon became full and flooded by monsoon rains and requests by us to be allowed to fill in these pits and dig new ones were frequently refused by the Japanese for some amazing reason they never gave. Throughout the entire Railway episode the Japanese were incredibly stupid. Had they fed our men reasonably well, and refrained from brutality, the Railway would have been built in half the time but it is now a universal fact that their main intention was to kill off as many P.O.W.'s as possible to eliminate any chance of escape by us.

In some camps when cholera first struck Isolation tents were set up some distance from the main camp and into these the sick and dying men were bundled. The Japs forbade anyone, on pain of death, to go near them, either to feed or attend to their needs medically. Left there in their misery and agony, many died in conditions even I cannot describe. There were occasions, however, when our own M.O.'s, already overworked to a fantastic degree, crawled out under the barbed wire at night to take what help and medical supplies we still possessed to these sufferers – and managed to save a great many lives. The Medical Officers did a magnificent job at all times under impossible conditions. Many were beaten up by the Jap whilst trying to prevent dying men from going out on working parties. This I have witnessed frequently. But always they continued to fight to save lives and bring what comfort they could to the needy.

Cholera, under reasonable conditions, is the terror of all, even when modern injections are available and proper hospital treatment is not only allowed but insisted upon. At its worst it can prove fatal within twenty-four hours unless immediate attention is received, and this with agonising abdominal pains. As a friend of mine out there told me (who had indeed not only suffered an acute attack but lived to tell the tale) 'I felt as if I was giving birth to a bath full of broken glass!' The entire entrails were tightened up, like a bowstring, and the victim eventually assumed a jacknife position from which he often never recovered. My friend who survived cholera had one remaining object of value left him by the Japs, a tiny photograph of his wife – hidden in his water bottle lining. He managed to prop it up by his head and, concentrating his thought upon it, said over and over again 'I *will* come home to you'. He did. I personally believe it is possible to reach such a disease ridden state whereby it is barely possible to get worse – the last stage before death itself – and then for the human mind to assume control and dogmatically refuse to leave the body, soul and mind being one. I am convinced it is not only possible – but a definite fact.

Those of us who survived the cholera camps via our return journey to Singapore now resembled a skeleton like appearance as shown by my sketch of a fellow P.O.W. Having marched fifteen miles from the cholera area to a rail depot, we were once again pushed into cattle trucks and despatched south. The journey to wherever we were going turned out to be a three-day period, during which time we were actually allowed to sleep all we wanted to! As I sat in a corner of the truck making sketches of my companions around me, my thoughts went back to the beginning of our journey which had led us to the Railway of Death. Our minds had been full of hope – expectations of at least humane treatment. And now, wrecked in body and mind the bulk of us were the shadows of the former shadows we had once been. Yet we were the lucky ones, we had survived that unmentionable hell but thousands of our comrades still remained up there, still to do the inhuman work demanded of them by their slave-masters.

Ultimately we arrived at a Hospital Base Camp which had, to our utter amazement, a totally different aspect to any other we had seen. The camp had proper hospital facilities, few drugs admittedly, but run this time (subject, of course, to Jap administration) by Allied Officers under the command of Lt-Colonel P. J. D. Toosey, a wonderful man. Even though the huts were crammed with men suffering diverse complaints and diseases, each man had his dressings changed daily, could wash and shave again and rest, rest, rest! To us, fresh from hell, this was heaven. Men still died by the dozens, by day and by night. Their moans made the night unpleasant but this, by now, we were hardened to. To be truthful, it left us cold! We had turned into iron men. Iron inside ourselves, even though still weak in body. We had survived the worst, this was nothing. The staff of orderlies worked tirelessly to look after our needs and food was far better than we had experienced before. A native run canteen sold extras, omelettes, tobacco, coconuts etc., and I, for one, was rapidly regaining my health.

I now had something like sixty odd drawings and rough paintings in my possession, carried from camp to camp rolled round a stick which I used to help me walk. But as the stick grew thicker I had to think of another means of conveying my precious records. Having only a blanket and small pack to my name, I carried the blanket rolled up with the paintings inside – one trusted to luck. I would get away with it. In spite of many searches, this I achieved. Now, at the new camp, Khanchanburi by name, I found many men ready to help me further the collection. I even gave secret exhibitions in the huts, as here we were often left alone by the Japs for long periods. Many Allied Officers asked me to do sketches of their loved ones from fading photos and paid me a few dollars in return, with which I bought extra food and bribed our black marketeers to get me paper and materials from the natives. I recalled that once in the jungle camps I had had to resort to getting a few rough materials from the Burmese elephant boy who brought up our 'canteen' once a month – a sheet of dirty packing paper and a sticky sweet food called Guala Malacca which I used as paint. But now I had ample materials for a short period at any rate and I meant to use them.

About this time I developed another tiny ulcer on my left foot, having scratched myself on a bamboo thorn. These long spikes are tipped with a venom that will, if untreated, cause a man to lose his limb and even his life, as was very often the case. In the space of four days, although I was able to wash fairly frequently, my ulcer grew to the size of a half crown, with a red hot burning pain that never ceased by day or night. For a while I kept the injury hidden away from the Medical Orderlies who, if they had seen it, would have rapidly transferred me to the Ulcer Ward, a long, narrow hut nearby that was crammed full of men in all stages of ulceration, several dying at that. This ward was the mental dread of all those with anything that faintly resembled an ulcer. The saying was, 'you never come out of that hut alive'. The jungle ulcer spreads with lightning speed, eating away a man's flesh with malignant greed. Eventually gangrene sets in and that's your lot! With over one hundred such cases lying side by side in tropical heat, the stench of rotting flesh was impossible to describe. Several men went insane in a matter of days. Ulcer treatment consisted of saline and a rough dressing changed every two days. Scraping clean with a spoon was also used. Very little anaesthetic being available, the patient usually screamed in agony.

Some patients still remained impressively cheerful, in spite of these diabolical afflictions, and one man in particular, his shin bone completely bare of flesh, would polish the bone of his leg each day. Incredible but true. After a certain stage was reached and gangrene was approaching, all feeling left the affected limb and gave a false impression of returning health. 'Beware the numbness' we would say, 'beyond that – death.'

About this time I was asked by an M.O. friend of mine to witness some of the operations that were constantly in progress in the Hospital. At first the smell of anaesthetic knocked me out but I soon forgot it as my interest in the operation deepened. I made many such drawings of all cases that I saw. Short of proper instruments, the Doctors often manufactured their own out of the oddest collection of materials imaginable. Ordinary penknives often played a vital part in operations, even hacksaws. Our Medical Officers did a magnificent job-day after day, often all night too. They saved countless lives. Major Fagan of the Australian Forces was a brilliant, tireless worker and much loved by all. By now, my own ulcer had developed. Fortunately the Ulcer Ward was now full and I was allowed to remain in my own hut along with many others in a similar state. Next to me lay an Australian, Harold Reid by name, and we soon became close friends. He turned out to be a Yoga and taught me much of this great cult. We discussed faith healing and he convinced me that my ulcer could be cured in this way.

The ulcer on my foot was now enormous, four to five inches across and at least two inches deep into my foot which was now half the size of a football. Little did I realise that this same ulcer was to save my life one day. I had been booked for the operating theatre to have the sore cut out. Many of these ops had been successful but many had not, the ulcer having re-grown soon after. I was dubious about the operation and finally refused to have it. The M.O. was furious but I was adamant. I had complete faith in Harold as a healer – why, I did not know. I just had. Each night after dark we would lie side by side, deep in concentration. Finally Harold would place his hands on either side of my foot without touching it and at once I would feel a white hot heat passing through the wound. It was agonising but somehow I stuck it out. Exactly seven days later the ulcer burst, splattering thick, black blood over everything – and all the pain went! When inspected by the M.O., he was amazed but said little, except to eye me strangely. From then on, although I could hardly walk, the ulcer steadily improved. During the day I would sit on my bed of bamboo and draw and draw – everything I could see, all that had happened around me during the last year. But it was mainly due to constant massage from a true friend Syd Thomas that I eventually walked normally again two years later.

In this camp conditions were better, mostly the Japs, several of them sick also, left us alone. Only occasionally did they tear through the huts for a quick search for radios, diaries etc. I dug a hole in the earth under my bed and hid every new painting as I completed it. The pile was growing fast but I still had much to do. Occasionally I dreamed of home but now I felt in total command of myself – bent only on survival and doing as many paintings as I could. I was lucky to have my work. Most other men had nothing to keep their minds off their surroundings. Often the screams of agony of men being tortured by the Nips would shatter the uneasy calm and we would wonder what petty crimes the poor devils had committed to be treated so. Probably they had been found near a place where a secret radio had been discovered. Knowing nothing of it themselves, had even so been given the treatment to make them betray their comrades. The brave men, often padres, who took the risk of operating a secret receiver, placed their lives in their hands at every step. Without the news of the war's progress we could have entirely given up all hope. But to hear news, reliable or not, was stimulating and encouraging. Many times we heard of massive invasion forces coming to our rescue but wrong as they always were, we half believed them. It was something to think about. The Jap, realising that news of any sort could tell of a Jap defeat, feverishly conducted a reign of terror to try to stop the news getting to us. This he never managed to do, though he tried his damnedest.

Apart from the usual run of events in the camp, which was now composed mostly of sick men, there were lighter moments of an almost humorous nature. Some of the walking sick were used on light working parties, bringing supplies from river barges etc. and several men suffering from acute skin troubles were engaged by Japs for such work. On arrival at the nearby river the men were allowed sometimes, if the Jap in charge was in a good mood, to bathe in the water for a short period.

Whilst the Jap dozed under a tree the boys would strip off their only garment, a G-string, and wallow about. Usually hordes of tiny fish would fasten on to their skin sores and suck at them until clean of all puss. Amazing though this sounds the skin would then heal up quite rapidly in a few days. It is doubtful if the Jap would have slumbered on had he realised that further down stream these same fish were being caught by his companions to be eaten as delicacies. A grim humour, yes, but to us a great joke. Men would try to get on these working parties just to obtain nature's own remedy for their ills.

As in all camps Dysentery was still reaping its toll of pain and death. Although bed pans made of big bamboo sections were available for men too weak to walk, those still capable of staggering to the latrine pits were compelled to do so.

A frequent visitor to this aromatic club, I had plenty of time to study the pain and suffering of many of my friends as they sat on the creaking bamboo pole that spanned the cess pit. At these places of degradation choice items of news about the war were often picked up. It was the only really safe spot to talk in. No Jap ever came close enough to take an interest in the effects of his own disregard for the suffering of man. For one thing, the stench kept him away and for another he feared to contract the disease himself. So we were left in peace to attend the wants of nature and get a lot off our minds, in more ways than one! I have almost tender memories of those visits, though I hated them at the time. Men, stripped of all dignity and privacy were themselves and many a true friendship was formed whilst indulging ourselves whenever necessary.

I have already said that this camp contained mainly sick men but so far I have only dealt with dysentery, cholera and skin troubles. Another dreaded killer was beri-beri. Caused by an almost total lack of Vitamin B in our diet practically every man at some time or another felt the effects of this complaint. Usually starting at the extremities, hands or feet, unless checked by large doses of Marmite etc. or some other form of antidote, it rapidly spreads to the vital organs, eventually causing death. Bringing a total numbness to the parts it attacks, the flesh rapidly becomes swollen to an enormous degree, distending and mis-shaping all in its path. The lower parts of the body were normally first to be attacked and the genital organs very often became terribly swollen. As an artist to witness such strange shapes fascinated me but the humanist in me was appalled and still is that all this suffering could have been prevented had our Jap masters used a little humanity in their treatment of us. In camps which had better conditions such as Changi, Singapore, various herbs and grasses were made into medicines, some quite effective.

Yet another side effect of vitamin deficiency was its damage to the eyes. Beginning at first with what looked like a mild conjunctivitis, it later developed into a highly serious condition. First the sight itself began to fade, with whitish spots appearing on the cornea, until, many cases I have seen, the cornea disappeared completely, causing total blindness.

Several of my friends suffered from this trouble. Some regained their sight after repatriation to the U.K. but many lads were left sightless for the rest of their lives. Beri-beri and all vitamin deficiencies could affect different people in many different ways, it all depended on your own personal reaction. Always, whenever possible, I would eat anything green (that was edible) or drink the water that green stuffs had been boiled in. I have always held that doing this helped me to survive many such illnesses. But for those who refused or could not digest such fare, the outlook was anything but promising.

Now, many more men were returning from the Railway area, flooding into the camps downstream. Hospital beds being now non existent, they were crammed into any hut that had a few spare inches of ground left free. All men bore the mark of cruelty in one degree or another and many had frightful tales to tell of Japanese brutality and needless vindictiveness. Legs and arms bandaged with filthy rags, stinking to high heaven, we almost cursed their intrusion on the comparative quiet and comfort of our own camp. Violent arguments, even fights, broke out as men who were in a state of physical and mental collapse and covered from head to toe with skin sores manoeuvred their way in amongst us. There were many cases of Pellagra – a disease where the skin peals off in great strips due to vitamin deficiency. This, of course, was regarded as only a mild affliction and these men would soon be back at full work again.

The only known cure to come to hand was concentrated doses of crude Vitamin B^1 and B^2. These were only obtained from (1) the outer husk of rice, known as rice polishings; (2) Marmite, now practically unobtainable or (3) the water and juice obtained from grass. (This was known by the natives as Lallang grass.) This coarse and often sharp bladed grass was cut by hospital working parties, brought to the camp hospital factory (so called) boiled and the water, when cool, issued to those suffering from vitamin deficiency. It did, indeed, have a remarkable effect and cured many cases, if you could get it down; the flavour resembled that of something out of a stagnant drain.

Amongst these men were the most terrible cases of ulcers I had yet seen. Until now ulcers were just another kind of disease but some of the cases now coming into camp were pitiful to behold. One such case belonged to the man who had three ulcers, each the size of saucers. One on each hip and one on his chest. He was put into the Ulcer Ward, in the place of a man who had died that day and fed on the best that could be found for him. Even eggs were available here from the local natives who were allowed to trade with us. Every effort was made to save him but in a very short space of time his wounds became so enormous that all hope to save him was given up. He 'lived' for six weeks in this condition, a living skeleton, unable to even lift his head up, speak or make a movement of any kind. His whole body heaved with the stench of death and, mercifully, that eventually came to him.

Though many, many men died from ulcers that had sapped and rotted them away, there were also many who recovered from them. I was among these fortunates I am thankful to say. Although my good Australian friend Harold Reid had cleared the gangrene from the wound with divine help, it was to be many months before I was to be able to even walk properly again. My own was now almost healed but to put much weight on the foot was very painful and consequently I used a stick to support me as I got about in the camp. I spent much time going from ward to ward and, under the direction of our own medical staff, I drew many examples of the varying stages of this disease.

The bodily system of most men was so low in resistance that it took but little to cause the ulcers to break out again. This in itself had a terrible moral effect on those men unfortunate enough to experience this but eventually the better food of this particular camp helped them to recover sufficiently to be ordered back to work again.

Looking back now I realise more fully that my own ulcer had indeed saved my life during the time I spent at that camp in Thailand, Tamarkhan Bridge Camp as it was called. At least two working parties of men had been sent back to the Railway area again, both comprising of men who had come south with us only a few months earlier. They had not been heard of since. Rumour had it that they had been made to dig ambush tunnels for the Jap troops to hide in if Lord Mountbatten's forces broke through. Rumour also had it that after digging the tunnels our boys had been driven into them and then shot. True or not, such things did happen and I did not see these men again, nor did many others.

Many men, put on the better food, made a good recovery and even skin complaints soon cleared up rapidly. But others, unable to stomach even better fare, sank lower each day, their bodies breaking out in massive boils and rashes. Once acquired jungle sores are difficult to lose and only good, clean hospital care would have had any real permanent effect on those suffering in this way.

It was during this time that I acquired a severe abscess on a tooth that had been giving me constant trouble. I do not recall there being any actual dental surgery to go to when in need of treatment but my tooth was finally most skilfully removed by an Australian dentist, Captain Winchester, A.I.F. The impression shown in the illustration 'Tooth extraction' gives an accurate idea of the conditions under which our Doctors worked and in which the men lived. It is a hospital hut containing miscellaneous cases. Men in varied stages of different complaints and diseases etc. The skill of this Australian dentist so impressed me that to this day I still have attention from an 'Aussie' dentist whenever it is necessary.

Many of my companions in this hut were far gone cases, too ill to stand up and too afraid almost to lie down for fear of dying. The physical picture was easy for me to draw but to express the mental anguish or apathy of each individual was almost impossible. But here and there I feel I managed to do even that. Some men turned into religious maniacs, doing everything they could to bring death nearer, little realising that by so doing they endangered the lives of their comrades.

So far little has been said of Malaria, an almost common complaint during peacetime soldiering in the East, but usually controllable and treatable with the usual quinine. Here, in the P.O.W. camps, quinine was as scarce as gold and in the jungle non-existent almost. Many men dealing in Blackmarket trading managed to buy quinine from the natives who had undoubtedly stolen it first from British Army dumps and Hospitals in peace time or during the fighting. Though many of the Blackmarketeers were bad lads in many ways, thieving from their comrades to trade with the natives, they also brought in much needed medical supplies for use in our scantily equipped hospitals and thus saved many lives. At all times the Blackmarket was rife in most camps – our old friends the Aussies being among the most proficient in stealing from under the noses of the Japs themselves. If you wanted extra food of any kind a 'Digger' was your best bet. They knew the habits of the natives and also the Jap guards. Even so, many of them paid with their lives for their bravery. If quinine was unobtainable the malaria rapidly advanced to a more complicated and deadly stage known as cerebral malaria, affecting the reason of the patient and very often causing insanity. A man suffering from these symptoms would frequently express himself with wild, unreasonable fits, screaming out dementedly at all hours of the day and night. He would stagger to his feet and literally run around in circles, and there was nothing we could do about it!

It was now Spring of 1944 and the Railway was moving

ahead with all the speed our masters could get out of us. 'Speedo' the order of yesterday was now the order of tomorrow, only more so. Men still working in the jungle camps and the railway sidings were drafted out to operate on the track laying gangs. Up to eighteen hours per day, and in some cases even more, was expected and demanded of these unfortunates, the sick along with the half-fit – for now no fit men remained. All were either physically or mentally sick. And as the nightmare continued up country we, the more fortunate, along with a few others, were moved back even further south. Most of our party could barely walk upright but many less fortunate ones had been forced to stay and work up country in a similar condition. We were indeed the lucky ones. We travelled by truck and rail, passing over several great bridges built by P.O.W.'s at the cost of many lives. Such a bridge was Wampoh – almost a mile long and 300 ft. high, entirely built with tree trunks. A great engineering feat.

Nearby, varied working parties laboured on either extending or repairing parts of the track or maintaining road conditions. These were also lucky men to a degree as Jap overseers in this area were not as 'Speedo' minded as further up country. The men on such parties were the 'old crocks', not old in age but in body and spirit. Men who had probably done many months on the Railway before being returned as dying. But somehow many of them had recovered. Numbers of Aussies amongst them, tough as old rope, they refused to die and dragged out each new day, doing as little as they could get away with (as we all did), not wishing to help the Nips with their war effort. Some men even up to their ears in rackets of all kinds, some of the unscrupulous ones, would brew up an imitation coffee made with burnt rice and Guala Malacca. This they would sell to their comrades at between two and five cents per cup. By this time everyone who could was on the 'make'. Very few gave anything to anyone. It was dog eat dog.

Along the track that ran south to Singapore many camps dotted the line and jungle fringe. Into one of these our little party was duly deposited to await further conveyance. We were all walking skeletons by this time. Frequently I would count my ribs to check on correct anatomy for my sketches. To sit even on soft ground was painful as your thigh bones were only covered by a layer of skin. Consequently great raw patches soon turned again into sores. In this new camp were many natives; Indians, Malays, Chinese etc., dying from dysentery. Our Jap guard told us that to help or feed them would be death to us (whether by his gun or the disease he did not say). These poor wretches crawled to our feet when the Jap had gone, begging for food or water. There were no cooks in this camp but a quantity of rice and a few vegetables. Two others in our party and myself set to work to make a crude meal. We made more than was needed for ourselves and then distributed the remainder to our native fellow sufferers. At night we slept alongside them, oblivious of any fear of contaminations, simply dead weary and exhausted. By morning many of our native companions were dead. That was the only time I ever cooked rice – I hoped it was my last.

I have explained several times the conditions of the latrines, bore holes etc. Comprising layers of bamboo protruding over the edge of a ten foot pit, the contents of which heaved and teamed with bacteria, these death traps were our only so called sanitation. As I have already stated, by a Jap order we were not allowed to fill them in. God knows why – we never found out.

Many poor devils staggering in the dark at night to use same, frequently fell headlong in and were either drowned or died later from shock. I personally had a narrow escape when, on one occasion, my injured left foot, heavily bandaged, gave way beneath me and I went up to my thigh. Fortunately for me a comrade saw my plight and hauled me out in time. I did not feel clean for months later and even when, later in Changi, water was plentiful, I always scrubbed my left leg more than the rest of my body.

Surviving several days at the native camp we were at last moved on to yet another base camp nearer to Ban Pong. Here the death roll was fantastic. Originally a supply depot for the Rail head the fit men working here had all been taken for work up country, leaving only a handful of sick behind to operate the camp. With the coming of cholera and other epidemics, sick men had flooded into the camp for treatment – or to die. Mostly they died and the Padre was left to bury them day after day, often with mass burials. I, like most of us, was completely hardened in every way to such happenings, unless a good friend was involved and then our thoughts quite often were 'he is better out of it'.

In most of the camps up country and in other areas, British and Allied Officers did a good job in organising sick pay and food for those in dire need. To them I give full credit. Their job was never easy but a few officers, it has been said, failed their men. On this I make no comment, except to suggest to the reader that he ask a few men who survived those days. I believe they will get a truthful answer – if they really want one.

CHAPTER 9

BACK TO SINGAPORE

Suddenly our small party became a big company. Japs screaming round the camp one bright morning, hustled us out of our
huts onto the parade ground and straight into waiting trucks.
God! I thought to myself, 'the bastards are taking us back up
country'. As the rumour travelled like wild fire, men wept,
unable to stand the shock. But we were wrong. This time we
were headed for Singapore. A Jap guard actually said so.

Our journey down the Malay Peninsular was much the
same as the journey up – except that this time we hardly
noticed the privations and confined space. To us it was heaven.
We almost felt like free men. I know I did. Now, I thought, I
will be able to complete my collection.

On this trip we were allowed to wash occasionally when the
train stopped at a station, by means of the locomotive water
towers.

Before leaving Singapore to come up country I had hidden
several paintings of the Malayan Campaign and with me I now
had about fifty or sixty rough sketches hidden, as always, in
my blanket roll. When in a decent camp again I planned to
carry on with my work, the work that had given me the courage
to travel the Valley of the Shadow – and survive.

On arrival in Singapore we were taken to what had been
Selerang Barracks, the scene of the 'great defiance'. The beauty
of this lovely part of the Island caused me to do the impression
seen in 'Back to Changi'. The scene depicts two parties of
P.O.W.'s pulling trailers of kit and equipment belonging to
Officers, who, bless 'em, had managed to stay behind in
Changi for the duration of the 'Railway' period.

Some of them had either used rank or influence to escape the
terror of going up country and lived in comparative luxury in
Singapore. Paid by the Jap, whether they worked or not, the

only work many of them did was to tend their own gardens, growing extra vegetables for their own use. Many of them at first disbelieved our stories of the Death Railway, so used to easy living had they become. There are still a few who will deny the truth of these pages for they 'experienced it not'. Fortunately they were in the minority. Their household kit, even as P.O.W.'s, was a mass of pompous, unnecessary luxury compared to the other ranks single blanket and a few other vital essentials. When moved to a different camp it was the O.R.'s who pulled their trailers and fetched and waited on them. Men who had already done their bit up country!

Now with the return to civilisation the great job began by our ever conscientious doctors to rebuild our shattered frames and rehabilitate us to something of a decent degree. Disinfestors were set up to 'delouse' our few remaining garments and blankets. Consisting of steam ovens of a crude nature, the idea was to kill the lice and bugs that had now become our permanent parasites, by steam heat. To a large extent this was successful but the jungle bugs are tough, and many survived to live and copulate again. We never really ever got rid of them. Morally, however, it helped us to at least feel clean. Once again we began to act like human beings. I was soon moved to Sime Road Camp – on another part of the Island. Here it was absolute heaven as compared to up country. The food, if not marvellous, was reasonably plentiful. Many hard lessons had been learnt by our Officers and now the rations were issued rather than hoarded – though there were still those who could not quite stand the sight of an O.R. eating his fill. Every possible means was now used to grow more food for our own consumption, and to feed the Nips too. There was always talk of Red Cross parcels arriving. We saw but little of these, mostly being confiscated by the Japs for their own troops. Occasionally an issue of clothes was made but much of this was civilian stuff – from the Lord knows where. By now, you either made your own footwear, native fashion, or you went barefoot.

Almost three years on a rice diet was now showing itself in our figures in a variety of ways. Even the fittest of us, and very few of us were anything like fit, showed these symptoms in one way or another. My sketch 'Rice and its effects' illustrates the weird shapes and postures caused by our starch intake. Weakness of the spine caused men to adopt a permanent stoop with a protruding pot belly – or those working in a cookhouse, whether they ate more than us or not, rapidly became bloated with excess fat that soon warned of beri-beri.

Other men, the type who could never put on weight, looked like telegraph poles that had warped. We all adopted the native way of sitting down, without chairs or tables in most camps. This was the most practical posture and very relaxing. By now most of us *were* natives, only of a slightly lower order I sometimes feel. The native had his pride in his heritage. Had we still a heritage left? We often wondered. Being now almost recovered in health, so far as was possible, I was working constantly at my paintings. We had several weeks of rest except for occasional light camp jobs and during every hour I could find I worked incessantly at the collection which now numbered a hundred or more. Many good friends of mine brought me materials, paper etc., and always kept watch for me as I painted.

During this time I found many good Australian friends who helped me in several ways. There was a camp theatre and I was called in to assist with publicity, scene painting etc. A most outstanding Aussie comedian was 'Happy Harry'. I forget his real name but as a female impersonator he was incomparable. The famous Piddington act too was born here. This brilliant, talented man and others like him, were, I am happy to say, good friends of mine. Others too numerous to mention also helped to make life worth living for all of us and particularly for me. I will say here that the talent, understanding, humour and courage that was shown to me personally by a great many kind souls in the Death Camps and also afterwards in the comparative peace of Changi, both encouraged and inspired me to fight my own adverse conditions and struggle to put on living record the great story of their own lives – and deaths. I sincerely believe that in spite of all that happened no man gave his life in vain, nothing they did was wasted. Their bodies may lie in a far off field but their spirits live today, perhaps in new bodies, to inspire and help those youthful ones amongst us now.

To those of us who had survived the Railway and had now returned to a higher level of life again, a level which, it is important to stress, had been thought to be rock bottom only three years before, a new approach to life had also been granted to us. Granted by that great God – experience. Though many of us knew it not at the time, our minds had either taken a great step forward or backward. None had stood still. The individual man within himself had by now either fully accepted facts as he knew them to be or lived in a dream world of his own. The Australian always fascinated me as a personality, though outwardly tough and often rugged in appearance he usually had a sensitivity that took him through difficult situations with an aplomb that was self-contained and self-supporting.

Generous to all and sundry, usually kind to those he trusted, he could be just as hard on those he despised – namely, the 'phoney'. 'Call me a bastard to my face, as long as you wear a smile' was his immortal quote, and that, I always felt, was your Aussie at all levels of life. A straight talking, hard working opportunist with a heart of gold. By great contrast to these characters were the phlegmatic and somewhat dispassionate Dutchmen, disliked by some on account of apparent laziness but really because the Dutch have a deeper feeling about some things than other nations and do not make friends easily. I was fortunate to have several good friends among their numbers. Indeed, I owe it to the ingenuity and skill of some Asiatic Dutch boys who had been brought from Java to Singapore that I learned to make colours from nature's own sources. Many of them competent artists, they already knew many secrets of jungle life which they imparted to me. I am most grateful for their help and advice.

Though not many Americans were actually on the Death Railway, there was a small party of Yanks who had been captured at sea and brought to our theatre of operation for the duration. At first they were treated better than us, but not for long. I first met them at a transit camp in Thailand. Four in all, names forgotten now I fear, but having just received an

American Red Cross parcel, they immediately shared out the entire contents with those Allied P.O.W.'s around them. Stupid mugs, some of us called them under our breaths. Greed now being the order of the day, but mostly we loved them for their selflessness. Get a bad Yank and you really have a bad one but on the whole they are great people – not unlike the Aussie in outlook. They will work the clock round for a worthwhile cause but they must have a good reason for so doing. Our story was theirs in the Phillippines and other parts of the South Seas. They knew the Jap – backwards – and had no illusions as to their fate, as unfortunately we still had. They told us bluntly, 'those little bastards will cut your eyes out if you give 'em the chance – play it safe, boy.' I never forgot their words. I never planned to be a hero, heroes died young. Too often for my liking – and I meant to stay alive as long as it took me to achieve my life's ambition, to be a successful war artist.

Life at Sime Road Camp, Singapore, was, as has been said before, something of a recuperative nature so far as living conditions were concerned. It was only to be a short spell of rest as we found out later, but while it lasted it was good. Rarely interfered with by the Nip guards, the contrast of actually being able to sit down openly near a Jap Guard Hut without suffering a merciless beating up for doing nothing took a while to get used to. I personally still distrusted our captors in the extreme and preferred to do my sitting down in the secluded areas of the camp where I could work in comfort. I was now inundated with requests by comrades, officers and even Japs to draw portraits of themselves. With entertainment not only allowed but encouraged I suppose I became a sort of novelty. All told I must have done hundreds of sketches of wives, girl friends and children of many nationalities, a great experience for me. I was fortunate in still having a good, if stained, photo of some of my own family. Unmarried myself at that time, my Father and Mother (though Mother had died when I was eleven) and also my very dear Step-mother occupied my thoughts constantly. On my first night ashore in Singapore before the war had commenced, a brilliant vision of all three of them had appeared before me in full colour. This wonderful mind picture had remained with me ever since and had convinced me that no matter what happened I would survive. It was during those dark, deep days abroad that the spiritualist within me was to be born in full. I have never looked back since in my beliefs, nor could I ever do so. I met many other men equally inspired and enlightened in many camps and some also in Sime Road Camp. We had many great talks together.

The majority of us now, though outwardly putting on weight again and possessing a beautiful sun tan to make us look fit and healthy, were beginning to show other signs of the appalling strain of up country conditions. We broke out in great rashes, boils or developed twitching habits. Many found sleep impossible. Nerves got out of hand and fights broke out. We had rarely had it so good and yet we began to get restless. Men began to get greedy again about personal belongings; arguments broke out over the possession of trivial items and a phase of petty thieving swept through the camp. Camp Military Police were organised to control such elements and punishment was swift and often out of proportion to the crime. Little psychology was used in solving these matters. Not realising that the effects of up country had played havoc with our nerves, vicious penalties such as chaining a man to a wall for twenty-four hours at a time, a bucket in front of him for the use of nature, was frequently used on sick men. These penalties were designed and enforced by the M.P. Dept. Solitary confinement was also used many times and also extra heavy work in the midday sun under guard. Some of these men may have deserved such treatment but many did not.

Though merely an observer of such doings I can vouch for the truth of these acts. Having almost free access to all areas, as now practically recognised as the official camp artist. I had opportunity to hear in detail accounts of many things, both from Officer level and that of the O.R. I became a sort of confidant to many, they brought their troubles to me, not complaining of same but often asking that I should include the story of their own little horrors in my records. There are too many such stories to set them all down here but I can at least paint a general picture of the situation. I have always felt I owed it to many of these men that my collection of drawings remained undiscovered by the Nip. Devotedly they kept watch on my behalf as I painted, often warning just in time of the approach of a guard on his rounds. I have shuddered since at the thought of what could have befallen me had a wandering Nip discovered that under the sketch of a harmless camp study lay an atrocity reconstruction of Japanese cruelty. My comrades made it possible to tell my own story in pictures – I am honour bound to tell theirs also. Their feelings, their hopes, their fears and dreads and above all their unbelievable courage. That was a part of my life that can never be surpassed by any personal happenings yet to come or experienced so far. The privilege of living amongst real men and being accepted by them as one of their own – to me there is no greater glory.

Our camp cooks were now executing miracles in the art of making rice a tasty and even succulent dish. Amazing recipes were devised, calculated to baffle even the palate of a West End Chef. Baffle – did I say? Frustrate him rather is the word I fear, but after the monotonous fare of the jungle this was living like a King. It was often said that a lonely tramp stealing chicken off a farm and cooking his meal over a fire in a wet ditch was a King compared to us. At least he was a free man and we were still in bondage. But by now with the food improving (though certainly not by love from the Jap) mainly from improvising local growths such as coconuts, Chinese spinach, tapioca root and sweet potatoes flavoured with chillies and a variety of native 'tit bits', we felt like tramps ourselves – King tramps at that. To me to be free was still to be alive and reasonably fit and able to paint. That one day the war would end and I would once again eat English food, wear good clothes etc., did not really bother me unduly. That would come but sometimes I even almost hoped it would not come before I had completed my collection. So saturated had I now become with this magnificent obsession that was my life as a P.O.W., I did not realise the work could have been completed after the war. Indeed, I felt it was better the way it was.

One of the features of Sime Road Camp was our Theatre, having been an Army Barrack's Theatre building originally during peace time, it lent itself at once to application by our own vivid imagination. We had, as has already been said, much talent in our ranks. Fine pianists, tenors and baritones and even falsettos were found among certain gifted characters. Female impersonators and general slapstick comedy abounded in profusion. Christmas, 1944, called for pantomime and typically 'Cinderella' held the day. One great character, a Sgt. Harvey by name, cockney throughout and volatile with it, was always a great draw. His interpretation of one of the ugly sisters was out of this world. A stocky, quaint little man, crafty as they came, but with a heart of gold, he could take off Hitler, Charlie Chaplin and many others to utter perfection. Working tirelessly he did us a lot of good. Always cheerfulness itself, tough and hardy, he became communially known as 'Charlie 'Arvey'. It was always the little people, the human people who won my praise. Their use of their own lives in the cult of humour and mirth was simplicity itself and therefore had none of the artificial veneer of the polished actor, but was all the better for it. These were the real men among us who kept us going when all seemed lost. Their optimism, though not always believing in it themselves, kept flagging spirits from foundering altogether.

1945 came in with mixed feelings. Every Christmas and New Year that we had experienced as P.O.W.'s had always brought with it a new wave of optimism and wishful thinking. The secret radios were still active and news was flowing, as usual, in fitful bursts. Some proved to be incorrect but mainly it was now obvious to most of us that something big was in the air. The general picture was to the effect that the Allies were on top almost everywhere but where that everywhere was it seemed difficult to say. Jap troops still thronged Singapore Island but not seasoned troops – mainly young occupation forces, lowest of the low. Unlike even the Jap front line soldier who had a certain respect for an enemy, these were indifferent and uncouth in behaviour. So it seemed that all crack troops had been called elsewhere – a small pointer, but a significant one. The pressure was on. But even so, in spite of these straws in the wind it was difficult to take seriously the fact that perhaps that very year we would be free men again. I had now been moved to Changi Jail area. Luxury camp of the P.O.W. era, luxurious only because of certain small essentials such as plenty of water to wash in, drink or shave with – and good, dry billets, reasonable working hours and good food on our standards. An enormous area of huts built from palm fronds and bamboo surrounded the Main Jail. Each of the officers' huts had its own garden of food stuffs, as mentioned before. Most of them went out to work with the men but a few didn't! Even to visit their men in hospital was too much effort for some of them I am sorry to have to relate.

It was during my stay in this area that my good, lifelong friend Eric Newman of Blackpool (where we both had lived before the war), came back into my life again. Joining up together as T.A. in May, 1939, both in the same unit, 137th Fld. Regt. R.A., we had soon been parted. Eric to go to France, through Dunkirk and finally out East with me, but in a different unit the 88th Fld. Regt. R.A. (Preston). Seeing little of each other during the Campaign or during captivity we at last found ourselves sharing the same hut. It was wonderful to have him with me again. We enjoyed an understanding that has lasted ever since and passed many hours promising ourselves the big 'booze up' we would have when we got home. This we eventually did and most of the first year home together was spent in an alcoholic dream I have to confess. But it was worth it, every single second. Never once during action or as a P.O.W. did I notice a weakening of character in his nature. Outwardly of quiet and inoffensive disposition, Eric had a tough, hard interior that he could thank his native Yorkshire stock for. With his help I was able to reconstruct many more accurate situations that he had experienced with his, and my, good friend Don Sexton. Don, a vivid humanist if ever there was one, kept all around him in stitches – and still does, I am glad to say. I trust the reader will forgive me if I mention names that come to mind as I write these pages. To me they were a vital part of my life out there and play an important part in my story.

There is one man, a good friend, a loyal comrade, who has

now passed beyond these fields of mortal strife, who I cannot leave out of this book. Jock Pearce. His picture is not good by my present standards of portraiture, but a true likeness of him as he was as a P.O.W. A cook in the kitchen of Changi Jail, he was a kind little man who came to visit me many times. I did several sketches of camp life for him and in return he would bring me extra food, 'tit bits' from his own food rations. Cooks got a little extra and this he gave to his friends in hospital. He also brought me coconut shells to mix my paints in and helped me in many ways.

Before he died a few years ago he sent me the sketches I had done for him as a P.O.W. to add to my collection, then up for sale. He wanted me to have them back for myself. I was touched by his kind gesture and have included some of them in this book as a salute to Jock. He was a fine man. A fine man yes – appreciated by his country? I wonder. Having been ill ever since the war, almost blind from his experiences, he was unable to qualify for a reasonable pension or compensation, due entirely to technicalities of Unit and Enlistment. There are hundreds like him. The words of Armistice Day, 'They shall not be forgotten' finds its own insulting level in the shadows of such men.

The daily showerbath is always a stimulating event in the Far East. In peace time conditions the drill is to have at least four showers daily, just to keep cool and fresh. To us, having been kept for two years in jungle conditions without such facilities, except when the rains came down, one shower of pure, clean water per day was heaven. The saying 'Cleanliness is next to Godliness' is certainly true to the extent that to think clearly and cleanly it is better to be physically clean first. When covered with the unmentionable filth of slave labour conditions I had many times ached for the touch of icy cool, clean water running all over my body. Cleansing intimate parts and bringing that almost delicious feeling of the sensual ecstasy that pure intercourse contains. This is no exaggeration in any sense of the word but an emotion only felt by those whose minds and bodies have experienced great contrasts and conflicting temperatures. I have known many rough characters express as much, though in somewhat prolific terms. In this sketch the men may appear to be fat and fit. Fat, certainly they were – with rice blubber. Fit? Hardly, but definitely on the up grade at long last. As another glorious tropical dawn came up with the majesty that is exclusively Eastern, we would trot out with towels, or the equivalent, and push and shove our way under the icy jets, revelling in the purity of the moment.

Whilst we had been away on the Railway, work had been started by the Japs to build a great new air strip for their long range bombers to attack Australia and other targets. Reclaiming land from the sea was a vital part of this exercise and then to build by hand with P.O.W. labour a six mile long area by about one mile wide. Natives were also employed on this project but mainly P.O.W.'s. Gangs went out from Changi each day to hew trees and rocks to lay the foundation of the actual landing strip. A native train, like something out of Toy Town, trundled loads of sand and rocks in various areas and then it was up to us to level off the surface. An Officer in charge of the party often sat in the shade chatting to the Jap Guard. No standing order existed which said an Officer should do any manual work alongside his men but a certain number did to take the strain off any man who was sick or too weak to work. Officers who teamed up with the lads in this way earned the praise and devotion of all ranks. It is a great pity that this cannot be said for all Officers at that time. A few still tried to exercise their full authority and rank, having remained behind in Singapore during the 'Speedo' period they did not realise the shattered state of the survivors of that episode.

There are some who will say that I have a grudge against Officers in general. This, I assure the reader, is not so. I have many good friends amongst ex-officers to this day who will, and have already, admitted that all those who bore the King's Commission did not always do so in the best tradition of humanity. One must realise that all men had now been reduced to the same level of life. N.C.O.'s and the Common Soldier, as we were called, accepted this evil and made the best of it. But some in authority never did. Even saluting an Officer was insisted upon, in prison camps at that! We were no longer soldiers, we were prisoners of war. Our army career had finished but still the old 'bull' remained. I have got to present this side of the picture if I am to tell the truth at all. It is all part of the story. Some Officers saw the errors of their former ways and changed their attitude for the better and became loved for it. Changi Jail was perhaps the most comfortable billet of all. The bars did not worry us. It was clean, dry, cool and free of bugs and lice and not overcrowded. The concrete walls reflected the sunlight all around the rooms. Good books from the Jail Library were available and it was here that I first read the unabridged version of 'A Thousand and One Nights'.

By now the garden areas surrounding the camp were under great pressure to produce more and more food. The Japs were demanding maximum effort to subsidise their own failing food supplies. Although we did not know it at the time, the Jap Navy was almost non existant and consequently little food, if any, was coming in from the outside. To fertilise the crops, human urine was carefully saved by using only certain oil drums fed by connecting pipes. This amazingly now precious liquid from our own bodies was poured daily into an old army water tank and then manhandled out to the gardens to be sprayed by watering cans onto the vegetable area. Was there no end to this pantomime? It soon became the butt of concert party comedians but eventually took its place amongst all the other abnormalities of our strange life. About this time I began to have a re-occurring dream. It seemed I was travelling home over the sea to land safely at Liverpool and eventually to be taken home to my own front door. There are other details but this is the crux of the dream. Although many I recounted the dream to said it was wishful thinking, eventually it came to pass in the exact manner in which I had dreamt it. The last six months of our life out there had very black moments and this dream convinced me that I was going to come through safely. Dreams are not always right but sometimes such things do actually happen, exactly as we have dreamt them.

'The Rat Hut' shows the interior of the hut I slept in and did a great deal of work on the collection in. Eric and I shared adjoining bed spaces. Each man in the hut developed his own little area of personality within the space of one foot six inches by six feet. The wall above each bed was usually festooned with intimate personal belongings such as mess tins (some beautifully engraved by the owner with Regimental badges cut into the metal) – sometimes a labour of love that had taken months of spare moments to achieve. Other articles of possessions would include a pair of wooden 'choplies' (sandals) made in Chinese style; hand carved and with only one leather or canvas strap to hold them on; probably a stained haversack that had travelled the jungle ways and other items such as a bottle of Palm oil, a homemade water jug, petrol tins turned into general containers and even a homemade dart board would complete the picture. The ingenuity of the P.O.W. was something that had to be seen to be believed. At night, large rats would fight to the death along the rafters above us and we would bet large sums of fictitious money on which one we wanted to win. Another amusing pastime was to find a large, fat bug, place it on a small ant hill and watch its final destruction by the ferocious Bull ants as they encircled their prey. Sadistic perhaps, but to us the bug was a foul enemy.

The P.O.W.'s ingenuity was also exercised to keep his belly at a reasonable level of fullness. Using an old wheel hub as a plate, he would build a tiny fire in the open, and boil up a brew of tea using dried, used tea leaves and a lump of Guala Malacca for sweetness, in a matter of minutes. Added to this would be a first course of snails fried in Palm oil or Ghee (an Indian fat) and possibly, if pickings were good that day, a fried mixture of chopped coconut, sliced banana, Chinese spinach, chillies and sweet potatoes. Utterly delicious to our palates – and so full of vitamins. When we were finally released we were told that we smelt like natives. It is no small wonder. In almost every sense we were natives. To adapt ourselves to the conditions that became our lot it was necessary to think as the locals did and exploit every possible avenue of succour that came our way. The Javanese Dutch probably knew the most about such things, as they found something to eat and cook no matter where they were. It was often jokingly said that they had 'two stomachs and no heart'. The former may have appeared true at times but I never found them wanting when it came to having a heart. We learned a great deal from them and without their experience our lot could have been worse.

Whilst on the subject of food it is a point of interest to explain in some detail the attitude of the average P.O.W. towards his food. To most of us food was the main factor in our lives, probably because we had so little of it. From the beginning the Jap had set out to demoralise us in every way possible. By putting us on a native Asiatic diet he hoped to reduce our morale to the level of coolies, but he soon realised that this alone would not achieve his ends. Other means were brought to bear, such as putting Indian troops (Sikhs mainly, who had treacherously gone over to join the Japanese) over us at guard points around our camps and compelling us to salute them at all times. Further more, these troops were allowed to search and beat us up if extra food was found on our person. Men caught red handed for such trivial offences were taken to the Indian Free Army H.Q. in Singapore and savagely tortured by them for hours on end. Many times the screams could be heard by those passing the gates of this infamous camp. It was therefore either a brave man or a desperately hungry one who dared to try to smuggle food he had found on a working party back into camp. Many tried it, some even died for it, and those that were successful had the tricky job of sharing it amongst their pals when back in camp. Forever under the greedy eyes of other less fortunate individuals. For the average chap who dared not, but just accepted his meagre ration, his 'Tiffin' or 'dinner' at night was the event of his day. All day long he talked hopefully or critically to his pals, speculating on how the cooks could disguise once again the everlasting, never ending, boring rice. In all truth, most of our cooks did a great job under trying and difficult conditions. Some robbed the men but mostly they did their best for all. I wouldn't have had that job for the world!

Having lost most of our equipment in the jungle Railway episode, when we returned to Changi many of us did not even have a plate or spoon to eat with. Consequently men had to eat in relays using the same plates. We soon set to work however to make new utensils out of anything that came to hand. A broken bottle was soon neatly cut in half by half filling it with sand and then pouring boiling water into the remaining space. A smart tap and a clean break was achieved. Next, to rub it smooth with sand and eventually a fine mug was produced. Handles were soon constructed from either wire or thin metal strips found on junk heaps. A half coconut shell would be draped on top to keep off flies, thus completing the picture. An example of this can be seen in 'End of a Long Day'. Spoons were often made from bamboo, or once again pieces of scrap metal. Hours of painstaking work would often go into such an effort and woe betide anyone who 'borrowed' it without permission! Flies were, as always, the menace to food, and indeed, our ultimate health. Fantastic measures were exploited to ensure that these filthy insects were destroyed without mercy and in many camps the standing orders were that each man was expected to kill at least 100 flies per day. A meal was usually, whenever possible, finished off with a smoke, if you had one. Canteen supplied 'stalk' tobacco. This was exactly what it suggests, the bare stalk of the weed. Long, dry, hard sticks of tobacco that needed hours of pounding with a rock to powder them sufficiently to make them smokable. Chinese cigars were sometimes available to those with the necessary to buy them. The usual price was from 25 cents to one dollar each.

The method of using human urine has already been explained but it justifies a further discourse on account of the many humorous situations that were frequently involved. We had been disciplined out of all proportion during the Railway episode. We had been told where to eat, what to eat, what not to eat, where to shit, where not to shit, and now we were told where to piss. Peeing being one of nature's natural humorous outlets as in the other function, the idea that such expurgated liquid could possibly be used to improve our food struck us as a great deal more than funny. These two four letter words are usually used as swear words, but to us, who had long since discarded anything that smacked of hypocrisy or false modesty

– to us, who had experienced every single form of debasement and humiliation – these words merely had a basic explanatory truthfulness and we used them as such. Few men went into a P.O.W. camp a hypocrite and came out in the same state of mind. But returning to the subject in hand, I would explain that in furtherance of the order to use only the specially provided oil drums for the demands of nature, any man caught not carrying out this order could be put on a charge at once and have a day's pay stopped. On one occasion I was on the 'piss' party and just as we were about to empty our containers into the waiting tankers a Sgt. came up to supervise this delicate operation. Inspecting the cans he pointed out that one of them was only three parts full (mainly because I had spilt some down my leg in transit). We were then ordered to present arms and fill the offending can to the brim. As we had only recently used the can ourselves this took quite some time. Whereupon the Sgt. told us to drink some water first – and get on with it!

There were two extremes of camp sanitation – the nightmarish conditions of the jungle camps and the type of borehole latrine that was used in Singapore camps. These were quite scientific affairs. By contrast to the jungle camps hygiene was insisted upon, even by the Japanese. Special teams of men were constantly digging new holes and filling in old ones. This helped to keep down dysentery. Also, many were fitted with a wooden flap on top which had to be kept closed when not in use. It was quite pleasant to find a quiet one in a corner of the latrine area, in the shade perhaps, and squat down for half an hour or so – just thinking about everything, wishing the war was over, that you were back home again sitting on your own plush lidded toilet, using best quality toilet paper instead of leaves or grass. When first P.O.W.'s we had used any kind of paper, even Bible pages (often reading them first) but soon Bibles became worth their weight in gold – for cigarette wrapping. Such was the value of the Good Book in camp. What beliefs men had by now did not depend on what was written in a book. It depended on what each individual man had in his heart. The words of the Bible may be right, we would say, but right now I need a smoke – and you can't wrap up tobacco in a prayer!

Religion in Changi was probably unsuccessful in the main, unsuccessful as a cult that is, because though Church Services were held each week and there were always a good number at the little bamboo Church that we had built, the churchgoing appeared to be merely an excuse to get off a fatigue or working party. As in the Army you were almost ordered to attend church, whether of a given denomination or not. Consequently, most men preferred to do something creative on a rest day (whenever that luxury occurred) or just 'kip down'. 'Backs down' was the drill whenever possible. We were all tired men; we needed rest not lectures on our spirits. Those of us who felt we had a spirit left within us elected to leave it as it was. Many of the Clergy were a bore. Those who had travelled the jungle paths with us understood us and these men we loved. But many Brothers of the Cloth who had stayed behind in Changi were out of touch with us now. Some did good work by visiting the sick in the Hospital area but not having worked beside us on the Railway they knew us not! There were the simple-minded ones who formed Bible classes (not that all who attended such meetings were simple-minded) but many lads could just never accept the reality of our life out there and waited for death to come, believing it to be God's will. Few men would have survived at all had this been the general outlook. Though a confirmed spiritualist myself, I believe that Clergy in the Army are totally out of place. Their very presence is a contradiction of the principles of war and, quite often, a mockery.

The appalling number of sick cases that our overcrowded hospitals strove to cope with was now mounting steadily, day by day. Apart from acute multiple diseases and complaints, general debility was rife among all ranks. Apparently robust looking men would suddenly collapse in a heap, suffering from nervous exhaustion, long delayed, and within a few days would be shaking wrecks. Those sick for long periods since returning from Thailand and Burma, suffering from such things as part paralysis in their limbs, dragged their weary way around the camp each day. On half ration, by order of the Jap, they cadged odd bits of food from their fellow bed mates who were either too ill to eat or even dying. A group of hungry eyed skeletons would huddle together speculating on the approaching death of a comrade and wondering if they could collect his ration before he died. Great work was done by the Hospital Surgical Instrument Staff in making artificial limbs from aeroplane metal and bits of rubber motor tyres. Many of these strange appliances not only worked but sometimes cured the patient. I know of one case where a brilliant British surgeon, Major Moon, is reported to have carried out delicate operations successfully with instruments fashioned from such things as silver tea spoons etc.

A very large number of men had lost whole limbs, either in action during the Campaign or in accidents on the Railway. With food shortage now approaching danger level in many areas, a Jap order was issued that even sick men must do work of some kind or they would receive no food at all. Consequently it became a common sight to find one-armed men hoeing away at a garden plot or a one-legged man carrying water and other objects for use in the little plantations that surrrounded our huts. Over all of us by now had settled a phlegmatic air of fatalism. Strange rumours were being passed from mouth to mouth. The end of the war was now only a matter of time, they said. Germany had surrendered. The Yanks had threatened to drop an 'atom' bomb on Japan. To our poor news-starved minds the rumours all seemed absurd. Atom Bomb? What the hell was that? Like something out of a kid's comic it appeared to us. What would the rumour mongers think of next to kid us along. On the other hand, we told ourselves, funny things had been happening lately. When a Jap Colonel had visited the camp recently, an Indian sentry outside the Jail had stepped out in front of the Colonel's car and shot himself. Reports of Japs being knifed in Singapore by the Chinese had also filtered through the grapevine but could you believe them? In any event, the Jap had threatened to massacre us all if Lord Louis Mountbatten's forces invaded the Island. We dared not think about it.

Quite often, when working on the 'drome' at Changi, a Jap would sidle up and say in broken English 'Remember me, Johnny, when war finish. Me not been bad to you. Me good Nippon soldier. War soon finish, then all men go home.' Little yellow bastard, we would think to ourselves. We'll remember you, mate, you can count on that. I made a private note that I personally would never forget the Japanese and neither would I let my children, if I ever had any. The sketch 'Reclaiming Land' depicts yet another working party near the 'drome'. We had been reclaiming land from the sea to build the airstrip when a party of natives came along, one of them wearing a British black silk hat, pilfered no doubt from somewhere. The Jap in charge, wishing to make the natives laugh, ordered us to work stark naked, to humiliate us he thought. It was now impossible to humiliate us any more and we gladly removed our G-strings or pants. It was cooler anyway. We had many times had to expose our penis and balls to local native women, all in the call of nature, so what the hell did this uninitiated Nip think he was doing? The joke was very much on him.

Unknown to us, our last week as slaves of the now no longer mighty Nip, had commenced. The previous week we had been made to dig huge trenches behind the Jail wall. The reason we had been told was because of increasing Allied Air raids. We had seen several of our planes for some months past. Three raids had indeed taken place in our area, so we believed it for a while. Finally it transpired that we had dug our own graves in readiness for the expected invasion of Malaya. Many times we had argued between ourselves that it was time Lord 'Louis' got a move on. What the hell was he up to? But now, he was almost here. It was unbelievable. For two days we were locked in the Jail. No working parties went out whatsoever. Then the flap was off again and we resumed our normal working chores. Had it all been a hoax? We could not know for certain. Certainly the Japs were acting a bit queer; all very quiet, sullen even. The tension began to mount again. Allied Officers had secret consultations. Whatever happened, we were told, keep your mouth shut. No cheering or letting go. We don't know how the Nip will react if the news is true. So they actually admitted it at last! The war was on the edge of finishing. And then, that afternoon, with a roar of engines, two British Liberators flew over the Jail, showering leaflets on us. We could see the blokes in the plane waving to us. At once Jap ack-ack opened up on them. Our hopes plummeted again. So it was all baloney after all. How could it be over when the Japs were still firing on our planes? Then we heard the Jap announcement that the Nip General in charge of Singapore had decided to fight on till the bitter end, in defiance of his Emperor. It was a further two days before he finally changed his mind and obeyed the order to submit to the Allies.

Then it all came out. The Americans had flattened Nagasaki and Hiroshima with two fantastic bombs called Atom bombs. These two merciful bombs had saved our lives, plus those of millions of other people in the World. For let it be quite clearly understood, had those two bombs not been used and a normal type of landing made in Malaya or Singapore, every single P.O.W. would have been executed! Of this there is absolutely no doubt at all. The Knights of Bushido always kept their word when it came to execution. They revelled in it. Much has been said by idiotic pacifists who only saw the effects of the Bomb in Japan and did not see, and evidently do not care about, the vile, unmentionable cruelty carried out by the Japanese during the whole sickeningly long war in Asia and his utterly inhuman treatment of all defenceless P.O.W.'s, Internees and Civilians under his control. His treatment of these people alone more than justifies the use of two bombs which were mercifully quick. Let the Japanese remember the scars left on their faces by the effects of the bomb. Let them be a lasting reminder of the foul crimes committed in a needless and unjustifiable way on those who were their honourable enemies. I remember the first day of freedom. I will never forget it, nor will any of us till our dying day. Lord Mountbatten driving a jeep with Lady Mountbatten beside him came into the Jail yard. It was our first glimpse of the man who had driven the Jap out of Burma and had been poised to sweep into Changi had things gone the other way. In one moment he cut through red tape and formality and held us together again as one man. In those few moments he gave us back our self-respect again.

The men around me were now no longer P.O.W.'s – ex-P.O.W.'s if you like. After the first flush of freedom they looked stunned. My mind flashed back to the day Singapore had fallen. We had looked stunned then but this time it was different. Before it had been defeat, now it was victory, but deep inside us we were too tired to make a fuss about it. The tension of uncertain news, the build-ups, the let-downs were now taking their toll on us. We hovered on the brink of tears and laughter, not daring to give way to either for fear we could not stop. Perhaps I speak for myself here, but I know there were many others like me. To try to control my mixed emotions I drew the picture 'Liberation'. I feel it typifies our joint emotions at this time. So much had happened for so long. To try to be normal and dispassionate about it all was temporarily impossible. Time itself would heal we hoped. Yet to this day there are hundreds of ex-P.O.W.'s who find it impossible to even talk of their experiences, even to their wives. The horror of those years is still with them. Little has been done by any British Government since the war to really help these men. We have been expected to drop back into normal habits again, to pick up the threads of our former lives at the drop of a hat. A few, a very few, have managed to do this but faced with almost indifference from the vast majority of people who thought only of the war in Europe and were literally blind to what had happened to us, many ex-P.O.W.'s have retreated into the same shell that was our only defence against those years spent in the Valley of the Shadow of Death. Very few people, doctors even, have the slightest idea of the grave damage done mentally to four-fifths of our numbers. The treatment of ex-P.O.W.'s in matters such as housing and rehabilitation alone was disgusting to say the least. And when the infamous Railway was finally sold back to the Thai Government, not a penny reached an individual ex-P.O.W. Almost Japanese injustice, you could say.

This then, is the end of my story. If I have sounded too emotional at times I ask the reader to forgive this indulgence.

The emotion has not always been for myself but for those who cannot speak out as I have done. I have carried this story within my mind for over twenty-five years. The facts were already written down before my eyes in the pictures I drew. I have written the book for one reason only. To tell humanity the truth about humanity. Not to assume the role of judge or even advocate. Not to stir up a hate campaign against the Japanese people. To this day I do not hate the Japanese. I could never like them as a nation; memories are too strong for that I fear, but I have tried to look at the situation as it was in the light of realisation for the truth. I personally learned much from my experiences. To make allowances for my fellow men; to remember that within us all is both evil and good. Just as there is day, so must there be night. It is the even balance of each that makes perfection as we think of it. We kill and butcher animals for our food. Only the half-demented amongst us kill and butcher humans. Yet each nation during history has passed through these stages of murder, violence and cruelty. This nation is not exempt in any way as the Bloody Tower can bear evidence. I hope and pray that the Japanese period of butchery has now passed. I believe there could be much that Japan can give to humanity, apart from trade products etc., but those of my generation will need a lot of convincing. The last sketch 'Reflection' depicts my own wartime impression of myself. It embraces the duration of the war, and is, I think, self-explanatory.

To those who have waded through the pages of this book and read, either with morbid interest, incredibility or sheer disbelief, or even saying to yourselves 'such things are best forgotten', I wish to add a further unsavoury course to an already unsavoury meal. You were not intended to enjoy what you have seen or read. Indeed, if you did, one might say you had the mind of a sadist. Perhaps to look at the portrayals of human suffering, the human form racked in pain and misery has given you some sort of sadistic thrill. Or perhaps I wrong you. Could it be that deep in your hearts you know the words and drawings contain more than a surface truth? I believe that here is the story of all humanity since time began. The far off times of the Barbarians, the galley slaves of Ancient Egypt, the oppressions by great Emperors and Kings who ruled with a merciless justice – or injustice as the case may be. The convict colonies of Devil's Island, the Bastille, the Christian Martyrs and even the torture and burning at the stake of innocent men, women and children alike, by such misdirected and ignorant representatives of the Law and even the Church who believed that only by inflicting agony and suffering on the human form could the soul be saved. If my deduction is indeed correct and this is your reaction, I would ask you further to realise that all I have set down in these pages took place THIS century – a mere thirty years ago – and parallels of these monstrosities are still taking place today. In all probability they will continue to take place until time immortal – in spite of civilisation, though on a smaller scale. There have been very few generations of the world that have not seen a major war every twenty odd years. But each time a nation is threatened by an invader there has usually been some great man or men who have, through their own experience of life itself come forward to weld the people together, as did our own Sir Winston Churchill. His great experience and inspiration to men and women of all levels, all creeds and politics, encouraged those who followed his directions and words to overcome fantastic obstacles and, in turn, inspired others around them.

Today it would appear that we are running out of great new leaders of men, that now individual greatness is not merely unnecessary but unpopular with many of the growing youth of today. The world hides behind the Bomb, the ultimate weapon to be used by man against man himself. Make no mistake, had it not been for the Bomb there is little doubt that millions more innocent ones would have perished than did as a result of its use. But having found the ultimate deterrent to man's slaughter of himself, humanity it seems is now content to exploit its shallow security with a dreadful carelessness that can only be the forerunner of its own decay. After the last war no other country on earth had a greater opportunity than did this Britain of ours to create a new inspiration that would ring around the entire globe. The magnificent and noble behaviour displayed by the British people as a whole was then the admiration of all those who believed in truth and justice. Can we now say that we are carrying on this great tradition? Have we passed on to our descendants the great principles we once believed in ? To look at a few examples of today's youth makes it difficult to believe that this is so. What really has happened has been a steady decay of morals, mentally and physically, nationally and internationally. Greed and laziness have replaced the sacrifice and determination of earlier days. Weird cults and discriminations have taken the place of devotion and discipline. To be proud of your flag is now almost a reason for laughter. A flag that does not stand for war alone but the welding together of great peoples – of all colours. A despicable viciousness has replaced the kindliness that once we were known the world over for in past times. These things are, in themselves, a bitter insult to those who gave six years of their lives and often their lives themselves to make safe and secure the future of the present generation. Twisted idealists since the war have procreated the idea that the world owes them a living and in their own endeavours for personal political success (and all parties must share the blame for this) have misled and misguided the masses. We, as P.O.W.'s had the simple fact that neither the world nor life itself owes us anything, let alone a living, rammed into our brain every day of our lives. Bitter as the truth was, we knew it to be true. This fact remains and applies today in every walk of life. We get what we work for and nothing beyond that. Those who have great wealth usually have great worries. All men have some sort of cross to bear and without that cross, be it physical, moral or mental, we turn into characterless zombies. The sacrifices demanded of us as soldiers and P.O.W.'s cut deep channels into our lives but every man and woman who has served their country and, by so doing, their own people, can at all times hold their heads up high. Theirs is the real glory. To serve in peace or war is of equal importance and I believe a great new challenge and opportunity lies ahead for the youth of today. If they have the courage and guts to take it up. To stop destroying themselves, to stop tearing down the great principles and banners of yesterday and instead use these as their own launching pad to blast off to a greater ideal that can sweep to the corners of the earth. But if this effort is to be successful greater hard work and understanding of each others problems will be necessary. Victimisation of colour and creed must be declared redundant. To me Britain is the greatest country on earth and it is always worth fighting for in every way, and I believe it is the human cell, the infinite original cell, that drives mankind to fight for life. To endure all, contest all evil and ultimately coupled with a genuine unbiased spiritual belief, achieve all. Age accepts it, youth can rarely believe it, but I am convinced it is so. If the present generation can bring themselves to think in these terms (and with their advanced level of learning I feel sure they can) they may then have the real lasting answer to their own complicated problems. I believe whole-heartedly in the present generation and its struggle for freedom and expression. Their candour and some-times blunt honesty is a fresh wind of change badly needed to clear away the cobwebs and the disillusionment that clogs the minds and attitudes of too many of my own generation today. The young cells are struggling in the womb of life; may the child to be born be a happy one.

▲ Exterior camp surrounding Changi jail

▼ P.O.W. building airstrip for Japanese at Changi

▲ Liberation day at Changi jail — Singapore now having fallen to Lord Mountbattens victorious forces

LIBERATION

▲ Spiritual feeling of liberated P.O.W.

▲ Artists mental reflection on his life since joining army
and his impressions of his inner thoughts

ARTIST'S NOTE

As one who was privileged to live in the time of – and under the command of the immortal Sir Winston Churchill, saviour of the free thinking world and all that is fine and true in life – it is with humility and yet with great pride that I have offered this story in pictures and heartfelt expressed emotions to all who may read it, in the sincere hope that some great good may be planted or revived in the hearts and minds of any individual who believes in the defiance of evil and the projection of personal mastery over adversity.

The cause and circumstances of the paintings reproduced in this book are of little concern. Many such things are still happening in the world today and doubtless will continue to happen until time immortal. What I believe does matter is that every generation has its battles to fight. To every generation it is always worse than ever before. This is the natural attitude of youth and even those not so young sometimes. But if the experiences of so many veterans of the last two world wars is anything to go by, the great lesson is, that at all times the good fight is worth fighting. To win or lose is secondary to the individual. I believe that to conquer oneself is the greatest victory any man or woman can achieve.

The hell and suffering of so many of my comrades in the prison camps has continually inspired me, in many dark hours since those days, to push onwards at all cost. There is no way back.

I sincerely trust that all who absorb the facts shown here will gain some inspiration and courage from the heroism and defiance displayed by the sons of this great heritage that has never accepted defeat. The parallel may differ in proportion but the principles remain the same.

'Man, believe in thyself, in order that others may believe in you. Fight to overcome adversity and the evils that others dare not face and so doing enrich thy spirit in humility and understanding of all things'.

BILL DUNCAN

I have included a contribution to this book by my dear friend and comrade Bill Duncan for the following reasons. Over the past years he has loyally and steadfastly believed in all my many efforts to get this book published, for our view on the matter are very similar and our aims identical. Never once has his confidence faltered when others have poured disinterest, disbelief and almost derision on the contents of this book and the principles it stands for. Thanks to the ravages of the Japanese his career and health were ruined years ago. Unlike myself he has had to depend on the grudging help of a country which could have been more practically grateful to those who survived the Valley of the Shadow. Yet, although often bed-ridden and constantly struck down with one physical relapse after another, his mental outlook has become that of a great far-seeing man. Never once has he bemoaned his fate or com-plained of his lot – being thankful, as I am, to be alive. His own story in this book will be personally treasured and honoured by me and I present it to you, the public, with a gesture that, to us ex-P.O.W.'s, carries infinitely more grace and respect than any medal or man-made citation bestowed by those who serve this society of ours today.

LEO RAWLINGS

I was crucified in Tarsau,
And again close by Hintoc –
I was whipped along the River Valley Road;
I was driven, pierced and bleeding,
With a million maggots feeding
on the body that I carried for my load.

Yet my heart was still unbroken
And my hopes were still unquenched,
'til I bore my cross to blighty thro' a crowd.
Soldiers stabbed me on that road,
But at home, I dropped my load
When Politicians broke my legs and made my shroud.

At Westminster, my poor body,
wrapped in linen of fine words,
was perfumed with their sweetly-scented lies,
and they laid me in the tomb,
of their golden-mirrored room,
with the other lads who had refused to die.

BILL DUNCAN

If doubts still exist as to what exactly happened in and around Singapore during February of 1942, it should cause no surprise. The official 'War against Japan' does nothing to clarify the position and the magnificent myth of an impregnable island has merely given way to other reports and accounts just as confusing. I doubt if we will ever know the full story of incompetence and ignorance that hastened the collapse of a numerically superior force to the Japanese 25th Army. I often think though, that we might have denied the Japanese their glittering prize if even a small amount of the energy shown by military historians and others writing afterwards, had been channelled into Singapore's defence by those in charge of affairs during the dark days of early 1942.

A new generation has grown up since then, and already the cry goes up that the second world war should be forgotten. To dwell on the past, particularly a part of the past that reflects little credit upon mankind, is a mistake. The creative mind must re-examine the past we are told and accept nothing that cannot contribute to a better future.

My view is that this is precisely why it will be a dreadful error to hide our past as if it hadn't occurred. And if in the end, through re-examining writings relating to the war, the young learn of the mistakes made by men that lead to war, and take to heart the result of such madness, then this better world they all demand will be very much closer.

If this story I'm writing sought only to glorify war, I couldn't go on. But I think that young people and not so young who ignore our recent past and believe that we who lived through the war were fools who richly deserved anything they received, must think again.

I'd like them to know about some of the men who were my

comrades in the prison camps of the Japanese. And I'd like them to hear also about people such as Tominaga, the Japanese Kempeitai chief and some of his henchmen.

And if they travel with me in spirit back across the years to the cholera camps of Thailand, and to a few other hell-holes we knew, that time won't be easily dismissed again.

Changi, a suburb of Singapore, had been made into one vast Prison Camp. The civilian jail and the army quarters, indeed every available bit of space seemed crammed with disconsolate soldiery, abandoned to all intents and purposes by the people who had sent them to that far away island.

'The Geneva Convention states. . . .', began one expert, and a few ribald comments cut his explanation off before he got under way. Many of us had heard about Japanese conduct in other parts of the East. Hong Kong was a recent example, and if one judged the Japs by that, we could expect nothing, not even 'medicine and duty'.

'What gets me is that we let these comical little so-and-so's beat the daylights out of us – look at them, they're not more than knee-high to a grasshopper!'

The arguments raged, and we had time to argue, for our captors seemed unwilling to show us their horrible side, the side we all secretly feared. Maybe after all things wouldn't be too bad? Simple soldiers seek simple solutions, and for a time, the only real discomfort was lack of space and lack of food of a sort we were accustomed to. MacConnachie's stew and soya links became mouthwatering delicacies of the past, and I even dreamed longingly of the dreadful army rissoles of past months.

Sad perhaps, but hardly things we could accuse the Japs of. It was rather annoying that we could find no further grounds for complaint. Soldiers love to complain. It is just as much a duty to complain as it is for a P.O.W. to try to escape. So I believed until later on.

We were poor judges of our enemy, just as those who controlled things before the Fall of Singapore had been equally remiss. After a period of time in which they no doubt decided that we must all do something for our keep, squads of prisoners were taken from Changi to work on a dozen different projects in the city and elsewhere. The residue, many thousands more, were kept at Changi, I suppose as a kind of mobile reserve, ready to fill the ranks depleted by some unfortunate whim of fate not quite clear to us at the time. But the efficient mind of Nippon had clear ideas on our future, mercifully unknown to all but the most pessimistic of our people. It's remarkable how many now state quite emphatically that they knew all the time what plans were made for us. What a loss they must have been to the war effort; what a waste of talent.

One particular pal of mine was named Tom Simpson. Tom and myself were included in a working-party which left Changi for Singapore. We were very pleased, for the grapevine, that universal news service that appears when men are held in captivity, whispered that food was to be had in plenty where we were going.

The information proved to be reasonably correct, for we moved into a wired enclosure close to a warehouse from which the Japanese were systematically taking cases of tinned fruit and other delightful eatables. Our job was to carry the crates and load trucks which took the goods to the docks. From there the loot was sent to Japan and to many other places where, no doubt, our enemy gorged themselves on the extras provided by Nestle House and other Singapore warehouses.

In a short time we settled to a routine. Pilfering of fruit to augment our meagre food ration of rice took precedent over everything else and we were willing to risk severe beatings if our excursions in the dead of night proved successful

Maybe our actions helped to change the Japanese attitude to us – I'm not sure even now. Anyway, where before they had been merely very troublesome Asians they now became cruel tormentors. Beatings were given on the slightest pretext, and a session with a Jap N.C.O. intent on reducing one's face to jelly by the jolly practice of slapping, was very educational.

Many times I recalled with real affection a school teacher I'd had at home six years previously. Compared to a Jap N.C.O. my teacher's hand had been as light as a butterfly's wing upon my youthful ears. Of course it was common knowledge that the

Japanese dished out the same sort of thing to their own men, but I never got around to comforting myself with this thought.

After all, a father may beat his own children and place the whole thing under the name of discipline, but he'd be in dire trouble if he went around bashing someone else's kids. I'm quite aware this may seem rather naive, but the truth is, we were 'someone else's kids', and unfortunately, there was no Protecting Power to see that we had fair treatment. The book had been torn up and flung away by the Japanese years before in China, so why should we hope for miracles?

Soon after this, my friend and I became involved in further trouble, the consequences of which were bitter indeed. At the time, we had no reason to know this, and when we did, it was too late.

Tom said many times that we must always believe in our hearts that the Japanese would eventually lose the war.

He also had a strong personal conviction that the only way we'd survive to enjoy that happy day, was by doing all we could to keep from giving in to the kind of life we were forced to live. Perhaps this is one reason why he and I got involved in the affair of the hidden radio set.

It all began when one of our crowd discovered the set in a bombed-out shop in Singapore. They gave it to Tom who had worked at one time in the radio trade. He was quite excited to discover that the only thing wrong with the mass of metal and wires was two wonky valves. Normally, this would have been enough to write the set off for good, but Tom had found some time before, while searching the Jap stores for food, a room containing radio parts.

After a series of adventures, we got the correct valves and soon afterwards, we were able to hear news from India Radio and from the Australian mainland. What we didn't know at the time was this. The Japanese were having rather melo-dramatic suspicions that a vast 'Cell' operated in the Singapore area, spying for the Allies and sending messages by radio from camps all over the island. Outram Road jail was filling with unfortunate natives and white men accused of endless fantastic deeds against the Japs.

The Kempeitai, whose deeds at times outrivalled the Nazi Gestapo, had swooped and taken away dozens of internees to Outram Road. Blithely unaware of all this, we went on listening when it was reasonably safe to do so, mostly on Yasumi Day, the Jap rest day when many of the guards took things easy and often left us completely alone.

Inevitably, the radio's existence became known to the camp

commandant. You would have thought that Winston Churchill was suspected of hiding in our camp, such was the agitation.

The camp guards had a spot check, then proceeded to tear the place apart in a frenzied endeavour to find the radio. They even emptied rice sacks in the Jap cookhouse and dug up the area around the compound, with no success, for Tom alone knew where the set was and refused to tell anyone, including me, no matter how much I quizzed him. I gave up asking.

'Kitchibu!' the guards spat out. I wondered what the word meant, until one of the others remarked with a grin that it could roughly be translated into English as, beastly.

If they'd been referring to the conditions, I'd have agreed, but the word was directed at us personally.

One wonders now if, somewhere in Japan, an oriental Noel Coward is perhaps delighting a Japanese audience with his singing of 'Don't let's be Kitchibu to the Blitish!' But to get back to the camp that day. In the end, they beat us with bamboo, with leather belts and rifle-butts, and kicked and slapped us until sheer weariness made them stop.

It struck me at the time as all very crazy, and I couldn't understand their rage. You know, the Japs lost a great chance to lower our morale. All they needed to do was, let every P.O.W. listen openly to the war news, and we'd have been certain that America and Britain had no chance. What with the Japs sweeping all before them in the Pacific, and the Germans in control in Europe – I hate to think what the result of a daily injection of such news might have done.

Instead, they treated it all so differently. There couldn't have been more of a stir if we'd stolen the Emperor's underpants. A very curious Race, the Japanese.

Then tragedy struck. Someone's finger, or perhaps just a fortunate hunch on their part, pointed to Tom and myself. We were hauled before the Commandant, and made to sit cross-legged with the palms of our hands held upright, in front of our chests. In this position, which few Europeans ever master, we were questioned about the radio. Every time either of us moved an arm, or allowed our backs to sag, we received a thump in the kidneys from a brainless oaf standing behind us.

The natural thing to do in a civilised world is to admit one has stolen something and hope it can be sorted out with the minimum of fuss. Unfortunately, our knowledge of the Japs, sketchy as it was, made this impossible. Possession of radios or diaries meant instant death. I'd the feelings though that our demise wouldn't be quite painless and so we repeated that we knew nothing of such a thing. In our hearts, we both felt that the Commandant would eventually tire of the charade and return us to the compound, battered but still free. Frustrated at his failure, the Japs sent for the Kempeitai.

'We must have been crazy to touch that damned thing!' I muttered to Tom.

'Maybe! but things have got out of hand now. If we tell these butchers the truth, they'll kill us the way they did the Gunners at Changi.'

Tom referred to the P.O.W.'s who'd escaped and were found in Singapore. Despite all attempts to save them, they'd been executed as spies when they were by right, P.O.W.s. It looked very much as if Tom was right.

'. . . if we don't tell them,' he went on, 'I hardly need to explain, old chum, what it means . . .!' I shuddered at his words.

We decided then that our one chance of staying alive would be to deny all knowledge of the affair. They'd keep us alive so long as they were certain we had information. After that, our lives meant nothing to them.

How does an ordinary man face up to a bunch of trained thugs? I don't know the true answer even now. But I do know that I trembled from head to foot, and told Tom so.

'So am I, mate. But we'll have to do the best we can!'

Later that day, we were chained together and flung into the back of a truck. Three Kempeitai N.C.O.s then sat on us, as if they feared we might escape despite all their precautions.

Talk about feeling inferior? Their every action surely showed very clearly that every one of them suffered from an inferiority complex so huge, it must have been difficult to live with. Despite my aches and pains, and my fears for the future, I kept this fact in mind.

Our lives during the following days and weeks were an endless agony of privation and brutality relieved only at night when we were left alone in separate dark, filthy holes without light or food, apart from one small bowl of watery sago and some water that might have been scooped from a drain. Every morning we were taken from that darkness into the light of day and driven from our smelly home at River Valley Road into Singapore. The former Y.M.C.A. in Orchard Road had been taken over by the secret police, and it was to that building we were rushed, almost like movie-stars to a Charity Ball. The urgency was the same, but the transport fell far short of good. Chained as before, we were, and looked like, Vilely Important Persons. But our interrogaters ignored our appearance.

For the first few days we were interrogated separately. The questions were repeated in such a way that I'm sure I'd have slipped up had I indeed much of importance to tell. I understand this is normal procedure by authorities the world over. The police state emerged later on, when mere words failed to produce results.

The routine each day varied little. As time passed so did methods become tougher and threats of violence became reality. We were handed over to the tender mercies of the lesser, more brutal members of the staff at Orchard Road. Still kept apart, we would compare experiences briefly on the journey back every night to River Valley Road. Every journey was less and less comfortable as we were by now in terrible shape.

Tom had tacks driven into the tips of his fingers, under each fingernail, and I'd been burned on chest and thighs with slivers of lighted bamboo and with the glowing tip of a Kempeitai N.C.O.'s cheroot. We had both suffered being hauled up on a block and tackle off the floor, with our arms pinned behind us, there to remain until the pain was too much to stand. Unconsciousness was a blessed relief.

One night after we'd been driven back to the camp we had a surprise. We were put together in the one dark hole, as if the Japanese felt it best to keep us in one place. But it may have been that extra suspects had been rounded up, and space was at a premium. Anyway, I was much relieved. Despite our bruises and our condition, we talked a lot then, mostly about our plight and about the Japanese character.

'Charlie Chan would find some way of getting out of this lot. He'd talk his way out of it!' Tom said to me.

Charlie Chan was a favourite fictional detective he loved, and the thought seemingly occurred as we lay on the stone floor huddled together.

One thing for sure, neither of us felt heroes. I wonder if there ever has been the character who takes everything flung at him by a tormentor and still smiles calmly back, his stiff upper-lip a rigid barrier through which no torturer can penetrate? How can a man feel ten feet tall with tears streaming down his cheeks?

And when a man screams in agony, does it help much? The scream is quite involuntary – an accompaniment to the awful searing pain that came before. That's how I saw it.

Weeks passed by and we had only a vague idea of the exact date. I remember the next interrogation for two reasons. The first is because it was the day we came face to face for the first time with Tominaga, the Kempeitai chief of Singapore area.

He was thick-set, with dark, cold eyes and his fingers moved restlessly, clutching a short leather whip. Obviously he was in an ugly temper and his rush of Japanese left us both wondering what was in store. Having given his orders, he glared once more at us and as if prompted by a sudden whim, lashed first Tom and then me across the face with the thick hide of the whip handle. My bottom teeth loosened and blood trickled over my lips. Hastily, I sucked in, fearful that the sight of blood might drive him to further violence. He merely grunted and strode out of the room.

Maybe he was so used to spilt blood, it no longer fascinated him as it did others of his race. Had I known then that I'd live to see him hang after the war, my joy would have made the pain in my mouth worthwhile.

The minute their chief was gone, his henchmen grasped hold of Tom and spreadeagled him on the floor, then three heavy Japs commenced to use his body as a football, kicking and stamping upon it like mad dogs at a feast.

The others took me and threw me to the ground. Variety being the spice of life, they held me while the officer who'd been a source of great pain to me before now demonstrated that he still had another trick up his sleeve. If my method of telling this now seemed frivolous, it may be that I'm instinctively trying to keep some human elements of life alive while I tell what happened a few seconds later. I didn't know at first just what he did; I only knew pain. A kind of pain unrelated to anything that had gone before, and this sudden torture seemed to be ripping my feet apart.

The sounds that came from my puffed lips resembled an animal being attacked by hounds. Maybe that's why I can't stand the thought of fox-hunting and the like. In the end, I was left on the floor, and although the pain was still bad, the first awful wave of agony subsided. I was able to look towards my feet. All I could see was blood at first, then I focused my eyes on my big toes.

The nails had been torn out by the roots, and indeed, now lay there on the floor like two bloodied snail shells.

We were pulled to our feet and made to walk to the officer's room, despite our condition. There we were told that the radio had been found and that by order of the Commandant, Singapore area, we were to be executed as spies. Two Chinese would also die with us. The words went on but I don't recall them all. Still chained, we were then rushed outside to the truck we knew so well. At the entrance, a staff car was drawing up. I gave a glance as we were pushed out of the Jap officer's path and got a shock. Sitting beside the high-ranked Jap was a white woman, the wife of a man interned in Changi Jail. She was smiling at some remark he'd made, then she saw Tom and myself. Her colour changed and she lowered her head.

I have always tried to believe that she was playing some personal game, maybe to help her husband's plight, but I never found out for certain. It still bothers me now.

When we reached River Valley Road we were flung into a different hole where two Chinese lay. We recognised them as two of the people who pilfered food at the warehouse we'd worked in. Their faces lit up when we spoke – and it was a change to be able to see, if only by means of light from a small window high in the wall of our new abode.

A surprising story poured from the Chinaman's lips. In search of tinned food, he'd seen a soldier (P.O.W.) enter a small room and come out with small packages in his hands. He pointed at Tom and nodded his head wisely several times. Tom explained then. He'd hidden the radio in the Jap store next to the radio spares. That's why it had remained undiscovered and only their chance arrival on the scene as Tom crept out had prompted the Chinese to investigate further. During the purge later they'd been arrested and under a long spell of interrogation had told the Japs where our radio was hidden.

'Why did you tell them?' Tom asked, 'now we'll all be killed, you know that?'

Astonishingly, the Chinese shook their heads. No, the little yellow men would let soldiers go back to camp. As for them, no Chinese was freed by the Japanese, and anyway, they had no families, and in the end, the victory would be ours, and the Japanese would be punished for everything they'd done.

Nothing we said would alter their belief, and I had to try showing an outward calm. If they could face death so well, it would be terrible if I let them down by showing my fears.

It seemed incredible to think that only a few short months earlier, we'd been free men in a free army, and the Japanese had been known only by things we'd read in papers. Now we were in cells waiting to be executed for spying. The trouble was, we didn't know when it would be, but we knew it would be early morning. The Japs had quite a belief in execution at dawn – part of the Cult of Bushido.

They opened the cell and took us out three days later. While guards watched we had to dig a pit in the camp area and I'd no reason to think I might yet live, when the task was finished. When they finally tied our hands behind us and made us kneel on the edge of the pit, facing the depth of the thing, I gave up and automatically ceased to think anymore.

They shot the two Chinese first, and I'm sure Tom must have waited for the bullets to end our lives with the same basic dread as I did. Nothing happened, then we were aware of sounds coming from behind us – odd, high-pitched sounds. My mind came back to life and I knew it was the laughter of our guards.

Our arms were untied, and we turned to face the Japanese officer who'd sentenced us to death. Unsmiling now, he spoke to us. We listened, still feeling the whole thing was unreal.

'You have been given a chance to live better lives by the Imperial Japanese Army. Orders are that you will be returned to Changi, despite your record of treachery. Japanese are kind people and care for prisoners. In return, men will not break Japanese laws. Soon, if men are worthy, many will go from Singapore to better camps in hills. Plenty food – good conditions. You work well and you may be sent. . . .!'

We hobbled back to the dark cell. Never has a place seemed so comfortable as did that place when I sank down on the damp floor. Life is awfully precious, especially when it had been within sight of vanishing forever. I wept with relief.

'Now that's real guts,' Tom remarked, 'your crying for something that wasn't worth a button last week!'

Three days later, we were sent back to Changi, and were given a great welcome by our comrades who had long since given up hope of ever seeing us again. We were sent to the hospital.

'God, you look terrible!' the M.O. remarked.

'You should see the other fellows!' quipped Tom light-heartedly.

The days we spent back in Changi were happy ones when compared to the ordeal we'd lived through in Singapore.

Our battered bodies slowly responded to the kindness shown us by the medical men. It wasn't that they could give us very much in the way of medical aid. The poor men struggled on with the bare essentials, and this despite the fact that the Japanese had gathered a vast amount of drugs and stores when Singapore fell. It was their tireless devotion and their eagerness to do what they could that helped me.

Stories had been circulating the camp for a time about the move to the North, and many fancy guesses were made.

Penang Island was one favourite, but I don't think we really believed that the Japanese would send men there. While some eagerly accepted the rumour, others treated the whole idea as a joke and steadfastly refused to be convinced of a move any-where. The pessimists assured us that we'd all die in Changi, and that was that.

Several of us lying in the camp hospital talked of the war and of all that had followed the Fall of Singapore.

Each probably had secret thoughts he shared with nobody else, but I confided often in Tom, who was my Tower of Strength and the rock on which all my hopes were laid. He'd have scoffed at this description of himself, but without him I had the feeling I couldn't have gone on. As time past I became more convinced than ever that this was so.

Looking at my body and reflecting on the past weeks, I felt resentment within me. I didn't think for one second that my injuries could ever be put down to War. Surely this wasn't warfare – even in its most terrible form?

Was I being punished by some Power for the errors and stupidity of the politicians who, years before, had flung away the chances they'd had to ensure a peaceful world? And just how innocent we all were, for if we were fighting a war against evil things, there had been long years of empty words and indecision to ensure that war became inevitable. But what can one individual do to hold back the Gods of War when powerful people plot and plan such horrors?

My toes were still very sore, and Tom's fingers would never be quite so supple as of yore. Even today, my toe nails discolour and drop out at the slightest knock.

To stub them against a chair or a door ensures that I'll have painful feet for weeks afterwards. But there is a lot of consolation in the fact that hundreds of my fellow men have no feet at all, and don't grumble, either.

One thing occurred about then which saddened me more than it annoyed me. One day, an officer came into the hospital and stopped by our bed space. He'd been in Changi since the surrender and I suspect the poor man was bored and not a little apprehensive of his future. Still, officers are supposed to hide such natural fears and show an example to lesser men.

Anyway, he was rather angry and told us he'd heard of our escapade with the Japs.

'Look here, you chaps,' he barked, 'this sort of thing has got to stop. It's going to do us no good to bait the Japs. We'll all get into serious trouble, don't you know? Serve you damned right if you'd been shot!'

I was taken aback by the outburst, but Tom, as usual, was calm and in control of the situation.

'Sorry if we've troubled you sir,' he replied, 'I assure you it won't happen again!'

The mental reservation implicit in my friend's words totally escaped the other. He snorted indignantly and strode off. I felt sorry for him then, and as I recall the incident now I feel that he was scared, and if an officer is scared enough to risk showing it to a ranker, he needs understanding.

In time, we came out of hospital and saw for the first time how much Changi had changed. On the surface, it might have seemed a change for the better. Grass was trimmed to regimental height and paths were neat and tidy, and a false air of well-being made it all rather confusing. Only when one studied the little things did the truth emerge. Changi was dying – slowly perhaps, but definitely dying. Men had far less flesh on their bones, and food was terrible.

I could now see why so many men hoped that the move North was truth and not just a rumour.

Just when we had all decided we'd be in Changi until we died or until some miracle occurred, the rumour became reality. Men prayed to be put on the drafts going North – although I believe there were some with good jobs who still wished to stay in Changi. The Japanese, however, took men just as they wished, and favoured none. Tom and I were chosen.

I don't think any part of the Far East has been written of so much as that which has been falsely named the River Kwai area. That, and the infamous railway received lots of space in newspapers and books over the years. And yet, very little has been told from the ordinary soldiers' angle. Perhaps we are not literate, or is it because there were many, and few have been chosen?

Briefly, two groups left Singapore, the first in August of the year 1942. Known as 'A' Force, they went by sea. The second group made up of two forces; 'F' Force and 'H' Force, left Singapore by rail for Ban Pong in Siam. Of course, this country had by then adopted the new name of Thailand and was officially at war with the Allies, but I never had the feeling that Japan received the co-operation she hoped for from the people of that country. Be that as it may, we were bound for Ban Pong, there to march forward to various camps along the projected railway line. Instead of rest-camps in the hills, we were to become white coolies, part of a vast forced labour gang working for the Japanese war effort.

Lies had been told and more lies added before we left the island of Singapore. Sick men joined our ranks because the Japs admitted the insanitary conditions at Changi and said that sick and fit men alike would benefit from the bracing air and improved condition further north.

Thus informed, we crowded into goods trucks, packed so tightly that there was no room to move and to try lying down was an acrobatic feat beyond us all. According to the record I kept at the time, our party had a thin soup during the first three days and nothing more. On the fourth day a bowl of tepid water with husks of rice floating upon the surface. By the time we reached Ban Pong, dysentery was widespread and men relieved themselves as best they could. The oaths from unfortunate comrades who suffered as a result of others in-continence were frightful to hear.

At Ban Pong we thankfully struggled out of our prison-on-wheels, but our joy was short-lived. This wasn't the end of our purgatory by a long chalk. Before us stretched a forced march of some two hundred miles, a march we were expected to complete in a little over two weeks.

It was still the monsoon season. The road we took became a mere jungle track and the going was tough.

We marched at night in stages of about fourteen miles. The rain was constant, sweeping down in floods to reduce the ground to a thick sea of mud. Through this sludge we stumbled, the sick being assisted by comrades. But sick or not, the Japanese drove us on, their tempers matching the fury of the elements.

When I was a schoolboy, I'd often visited the Perth cattle market in Scotland, and now I felt myself in sympathy with every animal that had ever been herded to the sales. Beasts of the field were better off. Stragglers were left behind, beaten to their knees and abandoned to die of exposure or drown in the mud.

Kanburi was one of our stops and by that time even the Japs had to agree to leaving some of the very sick behind. For the others, the road lay ahead to Wampo across flooded paddy fields and the same narrow jungle tracks. Tom was still in possession of a sense of humour and I remember him grunting to me as we plodded onwards: '. . . and to think I used to enjoy those stupid Tarzan films!'

We were miles from fresh water, marching (or rather struggling) on a route taking us away from a river. Water had to be found, and the only kind available was filthy and alive with mosquito larvae. We 'filtered' this liquid through grubby handkerchiefs or vests, hoping to reduce the likelihood of malaria. As if this wasn't enough, we passed over a swamp and leaches queued up to fasten themselves to our legs and suck our blood. It was almost impossible to pull one off until it had become bloated and satiated. They left behind smears of blood all over our bodies.

Further on, the land changed and the Japs stopped us by a rather big Buddhist temple. The priests, shaven of head and upright in stance wore saffron robes. I've read that in general these priests were pro-Japanese, but if this is true we must have been fortunate, for they gave us food which we ate hungrily. It was our first meal for over one day and the Japs had apparently omitted to include us in rations carried during the journey.

Once more we camped before reaching Tarsau. The jungle seemed to scare the Japs, who jumped at every sound.

This fear of theirs must have cost them lots of sleep, as the jungle at night is a cacophony of sound. We slept while the guards cooked and ate several small chickens. After three or four hours rest, we set off for Tarsau, a walk of some seven hours. We were shown a few bamboo huts but no arrangements had been made to feed us. Eventually, after desperate appeals to them, we were given dried uncooked rice. It took some of the fitter men a long time to prepare it for eating.

Tarsau was an H.Q. for the railway organisation. From this vast camp parties were sent to a hundred parts of Siam where they lived in tents or huts in minor filthy posts, building embankments or laying the track.

Tom and I commenced our jungle existence by going to Wampo where work was in progress on a section of line with a viaduct at one end and a bridge at the other. Hence came the names now embedded in our memory as Wampo South and Wampo North.

Rations were terrible. Four men's rations wouldn't have fed a normal person, and the lack of sugar or tea and salt caused cravings as if we were pregnant women instead of P.O.W.'s.

The deficiencies caused by such food are now reasonably known. They led to infection of the blood, chronic low pressure causing us to black-out if we lifted our heads or moved from side to side too quickly.

Pills to combat malaria were extremely rare, maybe two per man for a week. The amount varied according to the whim of the Japs, and our medical men protested, often in vain.

It was while we were at Wampo that I learned for the first

time of a strange obsession that was quite common amongst Malays or Chinese, many of whom were being forced to help on the railway. The condition is called Koro. Apparently the sick man takes to heart this obsessional fear that his penis is about to disappear inside his belly. Naturally, he holds on to it, refusing under any circumstance to let go. When sleep is about to overcome his resistance, relatives will take over. In desperate cases, a doctor told me, ropes and even nails are used to prevent the gradual disappearance of this important organ.

I wondered often what became of the poor man: I don't think the Japanese would sympathise or help.

The Japanese engineers in charge of operations were wonderful builders, but absolute horrors in the way they drove us on. Each day we had a task to complete, a certain number of metres of virgin jungle to clear, and so much embankment to build. Until this specified task was done, no man stopped work, and that went for the sick too.

The intense jungle heat caused swift loss of fluid in the body and even the Japs agreed to allow us tea, if one can term the evil brew we made as such.

Despite the sweat and tears of our daily tasks, food continued to dominate our minds. Beatings we relegated far behind this craving, and in time, the forage for extras led us to discover that even the jungle has secrets worthy of note. Plants tasted good and certain kinds made up in some ways for our lack of vegetables.

But of course, meat was the diet we longed for and because of this, everything that moved was eyed as a potential dish on which we might eat after work. Boiled snake, with the large python considered best of all, became common to us. Iguana is a food beloved of natives in these areas, but we found this rather odd creature too beautiful to kill. Or was it just too difficult? It's hard to say, now.

By the end of the year, beri-beri and other diseases were making the lives of P.O.W.'s grimmer than ever. And work became harder than ever, the Japanese finding that the time limit imposed on them by their High Command, was far too small. Perhaps fear drove them to the deeds they now committed, that and a disregard in general for everyone but themselves. The cemeteries grew and the ranks of our comrades depleted, and filled up by a seeming unending supply of prisoners from other parts of the Far East.

I expect the Pharaohs of Ancient Egypt built their tombs and pyramids with a supply of slaves very much like us.

We were moved on, towards Tonchan, north of Tarsau, marching for some twenty hours carrying any cooking pots we required. The route followed the rail track, then over level ground that had been prepared for extending the line.

We crossed several wooden bridges built by P.O.W.'s over water ways, crude and clumsy, I'd the feeling that very little would bring them down, for the men were adept at sabotage.

Tom and myself had become friendly with many other P.O.W.'s since the days in Singapore and some had since died. One tended to treat the death of a comrade with less display of emotion than before, but this was an outward show of indifference to cover up the grief which we still felt.

The Commandant at Tonchan, a Japanese sergeant we named Tiger, was tough and brutal. He also had the curious sense of justice some Japs displayed and his own men feared him as much as we did. He seldom tried to converse in English, but I think he often understood much more of our language than was assumed. He gave his orders through an interpreter, adopting the stance of a minor dictator in a small world in which he was supreme.

A further surprise came our way as time went by and we were shuttled from camp to camp, sometimes doubling back as if the Japanese had devised some sort of jungle network of marching men, all controlled by a genius in Tokio.

Our record of imprisonment in Singapore followed us, and we found ourselves singled out as men to keep watching.

It seemed as if our Kempitai days made us criminals still. Eventually, we were beaten badly for being slow to bow to a Japanese soldier and then hurried to the Commandant's office. He spoke of us as 'bad, bad mens' and sucked his teeth in the way Japs did when angry or confused. Not content with the savagery of his punishment, he ordered us to be put in the cages for a few weeks. This was serious indeed.

The cages, sometimes called Esau by the guards, were kinds of boxes about four feet by five feet wide, with solid sides, a bamboo front and barbed wire at the rear. The one they slung Tom and me into had the added irk of being built upon an ants-nest. We couldn't stand up or lie down, and for the first few days, we were jabbed in the ribs through the wire by guards every time we tried to relax.

Once per day, we were allowed out to relieve nature. The heat during the day was terrific and the ants, perhaps rightfully annoyed at this invasion of their homes, launched attacks on our bodies that we failed to beat off entirely, no matter how many of them we decimated. They floated in our daily bowl of rice, and it was Tom who prevailed on me to eat the horrible writhing mass of food when I could find no stomach for the operation.

After the passage of endless time, which in fact was later to be counted in days rather than weeks, we both realised that if we served the full time given us by the camp Commandant, we wouldn't live to be released.

Something had to be done, for already only the kind act of another prisoner named Jeremy, had sustained us. At great risk, he'd received permission to give us some small eggs which helped us a lot. But now, we were slowly losing what little strength we had left, and the torture of our cramped quarters was hardly bearable.

With despairing cries we got our guards to come near.

'Kitchibu!' they shouted, as of old.

I replied that if we were beastly, it was the fault of the Japanese, and I didn't think the Commandant would be too pleased if we died. Tom lent vocal support to my words. The guards pondered this rather odd assertion, but in the end, (fear of possible consequences if I happened to be correct?) the Commandant was sent for.

He arrived; watched us for a long time as if trying to find a solution that might prove favourable to himself, and yet keep us alive (for workers were desperately needed on the railway). He at last made up his mind.

We were taken out of the cage and returned to camp. No doubt he felt he'd prevented a loss of face, and after all, he could punish us later for daring to present him with such an ultimatum. We had been fortunate once again.

Shortly afterwards we were sent up river to Takanun. I fancy this was his way of ridding himself of men he wished dead. For we were going to an area where cholera had broken out. Cholera, that ancient scourge of the East, endemic of Siam during the dry season.

Our doctors had only one thing to combat this awful disease; M & B tablets. But naturally, they had to go much further in their fight against the plague. Pints of saline solution would be poured into the veins of sufferers every day but hundreds died painfully from muscle cramps and in the last resort, complete kidney failure.

The Japanese feared cholera. But even worse, they left our doctors to fend alone, and isolated the camp.

One day, after working on an embankment, Tom collapsed. A whitish fluid trickled from his mouth and with a kind of horror I realised he had cholera. Now, I said earlier that I lived with the idea that Tom's presence meant life itself to me. Perhaps that gave me the strength to carry him to the cholera compound and drop his limp body at the feet of a startled M.O. He was very understanding, despite the queue already awaiting his help. He saw at once how sick Tom was.

I was cursed loudly, but told to take Tom to the sick-bay. For the next few days, I was in fearful apprehension, for how could he survive when so many others had died?

The sickness increased so that the camp became one big disaster area. We dug pits to bury the dead, only to find that in a few hours, maggots had all but consumed the pitiful remains and the result harboured more disease. We started to burn the dead, building huge pyres of bamboo and wood, piling the dead up until it was like some terrible Black Mass, with the flames leaping about the corpses of men who not long ago had worked alongside us on the railway.

I went to the sick-bay to see how Tom was doing, and in a moment of sheer agony of mind, found out he'd been moved to a second hut, a long narrow bamboo-slatted place we called the Death House. Men considered to be dying were placed there and very few ever lived to recall the experience.

Jeremy went with me to search. Tom wasn't there, either. We tried the mortuary, a hut where corpses were prepared for cremation. Rings and other means of identity were piled on a table, and the dead laid out ready by two volunteers from the camp. Because of the nature of their job, it was inevitable they be nicknamed Burke and Hare.

In a frenzy of fear, I asked them if Tom was there. They shrugged, unconcerned with my childish display. Death was too old a friend for pity to touch them.

More questions, and one of the men admitted that only a short-time before, some bodies had been taken to the pyres.

'That's it, my old chum!' Jeremy remarked, sadly.

I glared at him. Later, he told me my face was lit with a kind of mad frenzy, and that it scared him.

Perhaps he's right. Anyway, I can recall only one thing. My wild dash out of the mortuary towards the huge burning pyres where, I was certain, Tom lay – not yet dead.

I think that in my heart, I really believed that Tom was dead. But my mind was confused and my body propelled by an urgency that bore no relationship to normality.

Desperately I searched for him, first of all amongst the pathetic bundles lying on the ground and then, with even more panic, I sought him on the piles of dead already forming a funeral pyre.

The P.O.W.'s busy disposing of their comrades must have thought I'd gone mad, but I paid little conscious heed to any of them.

Then I saw Tom. His head hung loosely over the edge of a pile of bodies, the flames already licking greedily at his arms and legs. He lay like a rag doll tossed upon a refuse dump, his eyes wide open and lifeless.

I think I called his name once or twice, and then I found myself climbing over the soft yielding forms of newly-dead men, my bare feet slipping as I endeavoured to keep my balance. Finally, I reached up far enough to touch his hand, and with the flames scorching my own body, pulled him towards me. He slid over the naked bodies of the other men and lay inert on the ground.

My remaining strength was negligible, but with some reserve drawn probably from my nervous system, I picked Tom up and carried him towards the camp hospital.

He weighed around five stones, and my own weight was probably a stone less, because of our different build.

For the second time in a few weeks the astonished man looked at me with his mouth open.

'Do something for him, sir – he isn't dead!' I shouted out. That overworked officer must have seen how close to complete breakdown I was. Maybe that was why he didn't have me put under restraint.

Anyway, he ignored me, bent down and held Tom's pulse while he listened for any sort of faint beat from his heart.

An eternity passed. The M.O. straightened.

'My God! – this man's still alive!' he said.

Tom was taken away by orderlies and my burns were seen to. Very little was available to help, but nothing seemed to matter except that my friend was alive. But it was to be a long time before he was out of danger. The day came however when I was told I could see him for a while.

I went with Jeremy to the hospital. Tom lay on the rough bed, pale and weak but with the touch of a smile on his lips.

He looked up and eyed me for a second or two.

'You left it a bit late, didn't you?' he murmured.

I nodded, my heart too full to reply.

The railway was behind schedule: the Japanese said it had to be finished by the end of the year and it was becoming clear that even more work would be required daily if this was to be accomplished. When Tom had regained some measure of health, he joined us once again on the work-parties, for with typical Jap heartlessness all who recovered from the effects of cholera joined others who were already, according to our captors, fit and well.

At a place named Kayu the conditions were enough to give us nightmares. We were awakened at four in the morning by guards shouting: 'Tenku, Tenku!'

From that moment, they knocked us about as we got up from our beds made of bamboo with rice sacks as covering. Bugs and lice swarmed all over the place, and I swear now that they fell in line with us and ate the same breakfast. A cup of boiled rice and a bowl of germ-filled tea.

The darkness of the jungle mornings caused us to stumble about and curses of men as they proceeded immediately to relieve their bowels lent sinister and squalid airs to an already distressing scene. The same scenes were enacted in a dozen different camps and the pattern of life varied only to a slight degree. The names of these hell-holes come back now to plague me just as the death camps of the Nazis must still live within those who survived them. Tonchan, Kinsayok, Hintock, and the base camps at Kanburi and Tarsau. One wonders just how much punishment the average human frame can possibly take. Certainly far more that I'd ever have thought possible, and it was only the advent of many years that brought to me, personally, the truth. That even when one survived the horror of the camps, the effects came home with us, later to venture into the open and mock us for imagining that we'd escaped.

In December of 1943, the railway was completed, and Bangkok was joined to Rangoon in the far North. Only parts of the line ever ran properly, and other factors assisted.

Today, part of our railway still runs from Kanburi to Nantok, a distance of some seventy miles. This stretch of line takes in the viaduct at Wampo, where Tom and I first started to build our share of the embankments and feel the touch of bamboo across our backs. The rest of the two hundred and fifty mile railway is no more.

The jungle, that ever-present foe of man, has swept every inch of railway from its path, covering up many staging camps and perhaps because nature is so much more kindly than Man, the scenes of Japanese torture and death have now been covered up and the jungle become once again master over all.

Many survivors returned to Singapore when work ceased on the railway, but for a time, we were held in smaller camps and provided maintenance gangs, ready to be sent to the line when required. Kinsayok had been re-built to house thousands of men from the camps further north.

It became overrun with rats, and the Japs told our medical staff that bubonic plague was rife. Naturally this statement had to be examined, but in the end, the rumour proved wrong. We set about ridding ourselves of the unwelcome pests. In the weeks that past we killed over nine thousand rats, but failed to prevent an outbreak of typhus. No treatment for this was available, and all we could do was stand by and hope for the best.

Between having men in hospital with this new scourge, and fighting the usual things such as tropical ulcers and vitamin diseases, one might be excused for thinking we had enough troubles. But one more came to join the others – this time from a source hitherto unknown.

The Allies had started bombing the area, and in particular, any trains moving on the railway. Unfortunately, they strafed the line, shooting up anything that moved, and dozens of prisoners were brought to Kinsayok with bad wounds. It seemed ironic that many who had survived years of deprivation should die in the jungle at the hands of their friends because of a railway they'd helped to build for the enemy. Nothing shows better than this the sheer bestiality and stupidity of mankind at war.

Occasionally despite the horror of that time, humour floated to the surface. One would have thought that such a human feeling would long ago have been extinguished in the mud and filth of a hundred jungle camps, but this wasn't so.

The new Commandant of one camp decided that he'd like built for himself a large house of bamboo with separate rooms for bathing and other pursuits. A wide verandah was also included and he gave orders that a party of men should forthwith cut the necessary bamboo and build it.

What possessed him to include a group of Aussies in the party remains a secret which he took with him to his death one day in Singapore after the war, but the fact is, he did just this. The Aussies were notorious for latching on to anything that brought discomfort or loss of face to the Japs. Tom and myself were also on the building party.

After a short time, while he assured himself that things were proceeding as he desired, the Jap Commandant left us to carry on.

Immediately, holes were bored in the wooden blocks we were using for foundations, and termites by the thousand were poured into these holes which were then blocked up.

For the next three days the work of transferring the hungry white ants continued and then the new hut was finished off.

Proudly, the Japs examined the finished product, and announced that every man would get a good meal. True to their promise, we had bowls of fresh fish caught by the Japs and the Commandant handed out cigarettes to us, his face alight with pleasure.

Our friend Jeremy got a board and some goo that passed for paint. Laboriously he wrote out an inscription in Latin and presented it to the Major, telling him it was a Christian prayer for the well-being of the owner of the new hut. There was a moment of hesitation while the Japs thought all this over, then the smiles returned and Jeremy was asked to hang his board over the porch.

Later, when we'd all gone back to our huts we asked him what the inscription meant. He smiled happily.

'It simply means,' he said: 'Lest the Lord build this House, they labour in vain that build it.'

A few days later, it collapsed while the Major was bathing.

As the fortunes of war swayed more and more in favour of the Allied cause, the Japanese became even more temperamental. We guessed they were worried about the change in fortunes and once, we were ordered to assist a trainload of Japs heading up North, where there were by now fierce attacks by the British army. We eyed each other with suspicion but was it just imagination, or did I see in the faces of these Jap soldiers a kind of wistful longing to be out of the fighting, as we had been for so long?

Arrogance still filled the minds of our guards, however, and an order which later was proved to originate from Tokio, said that deep ditches were to be dug around camps. Barbed-wire encircled the outer edge of the ditches and the prisoners were enclosed within this area. To our consternation, gun emplacements were then built, and everyone noticed that the guns all pointed inwards. They didn't fear an attack from outside and we were hardly in a position to offer much resistance, so the conclusion became obvious.

They were getting prepared to shoot us all down. The deep ditches would then be used as mass graves.

After the war ended, all doubts on this score were made clear when documents captured or found, stated that all P.O.W.'s were to be disposed of and that Japanese soldiers likely to be held responsible for 'unusual occurrences', were given permission to 'disappear without trace . . .'.

Life was much easier in that we ceased to work so hard. I kept notes as I'd done throughout the years of captivity, and crammed the bits and pieces into a false bottom of my water bottle, welded to the original. I'd always thought it a rather poor job, but the Japs never noticed the extra metal. Now I wrote on any scrap of paper I could find, and such was the need to examine anything written in English, the small book of church anthems belonging to my father which I'd also kept with me, was now passed around and read thoroughly.

Once, a Japanese N.C.O. had questioned me about it, and I'd explained that it was a prayer book. He'd nodded understandingly, and handed it back reverently. Now the lads chose favourite passages and marked them on the page.

We had very little time to think about God in the camps. Many of us were far from believers and others who had felt strongly, had lost their faith. Many sustained their minds by a strong belief in God. But I noticed that most of the lads chose to read this book of mine, and that each one was attracted to different words. I'd been given the book years before by my mother, but this was the first time I realised that a Christian book holds attractions for all kinds of people, most of all for men one never suspected of being religious. I note now that the passage marked by over twenty of my comrades was the following:

'For a moment have I forsaken thee: but with great mercies will I gather thee. In a little wrath I had my face from thee for a moment; but with everlasting kindness will I have mercy on thee,' saith the Lord. The words were from Isaiah.

Believer or not, one had to admit that some Power, and a very strong Power at that, had seen fit to keep us alive. And I fail to see how men could have lived on without some Rock to which he clung. I called that period our resurrection period, the time when we realised that we could really live on and see it through.

From God alone knows where, one man dug up a years old magazine of American origin. There were some pages of real pin-up pictures. Normally, soldiers will tear these out and think longingly of peacetime pursuits. We ignored them, and cut out several coloured pages depicting foods of a seeming endless variety. Hanging up in the hut were pictures of custards, turkeys in stuffing, and ice-creams of every hue. It was the most beautiful picture I'd ever seen.

Others gave talks on such things as: The ball-cock and it's potential, and how to distil whisky without a licence. An embryo lawyer practised his speeches on us, and a former member of a debating society took as his subject the question: Should women wear chastity belts during wartime?

Once or twice, the sight of a barge moving slowly down-river loaded with corpses made us realise we were still expendable. The barges of the dead. Men from various camps who were no longer of value to the Japs. I was now twenty-four years of age, but in the short period of three years had experienced so much, I felt and must have looked, a much older man.

We moved south to Kanburi, the big base camp where the desperately sick received every possible aid from the medical staff. Wild rumours abounded that the war was nearing its end, and that we were due to return to Changi.

We wanted to believe this. After over three years of privation a man's hopes aren't easily raised. But the physical body had refused to bow down before the worst the Japs could fling our way. In the whole history of mankind, the canvas of life has been illuminated by thousands of illustrations proving this fact.

Now it had helped us survive. Yet a great danger remained. As the fortunes of war swung our way, it was always on the cards that one tiny incident might inflame our enemy and that we would all be slaughtered. Our luck held and within a few weeks we were on the move again, this time down through Jahore and into Singapore once again.

Changi again. This time, it was like coming home, for I don't really think I'd been at all certain that I'd ever live to return from the camps up north.

Lying on my stomach at night so that my raw buttocks were less painful, I prayed that nothing would happen to me at that late stage. A lot of changes occurred. No longer did the Japs insist that we bow to them. And they all seemed preoccupied with some new worry which made them ignore us more and more.

Then we heard of the atom bomb dropped on Japan. Food improved, and for the first time, drugs were offered from the stores that had never before been available.

After the years of threats and violence and the continued assertions that no prisoner would survive, it was hard to accept the truth. The camps, for so long isolated from the rest of the world became prisons without bars. The gates were unlocked but few of us tried to leave.

Perhaps we feared some Japanese trick. It wasn't easy to realise that the killing was over. Our minds, for so long accustomed to fencing with the Japs didn't quite take it all in.

In the midst of all this, Tom still managed to get into bother, although it was, to my mind, a shocking incident that does no credit to the British Army.

Full of emotion because of the terrific news, he had words with a Major in the camp. Our own officers were responsible to the Japs for the smooth running of the P.O.W. lines, and the Major objected to Tom's manner.

Perhaps he feared that Tom's open contempt for the Japs might still lead to trouble. They were still armed and in a very touchy mood. He charged Tom with refusing to obey an order.

He was put on the carpet and awarded five days in the cells at Changi Jail.

That's one memory of the last day of war. Tom flung in jail by our own people. I've never quite forgiven the officers responsible. Maybe now, they regret it all.

It was all over. Very tall and very fit super-men from the outside world took over and we went over our stories again and again. Security men sought those Japs who had behaved badly towards us, and were puzzled in many cases by our complete disinterest. With wry smiles we tried to explain how ridiculous it was to put a nation on trial. How were we to know the time could come when the Allies would be on trial for using the Atom Bomb?

All these stories published about the dropping of the bomb should be read, not in the light of the present, but kept in a proper context.

We would all have perished had not the atom bomb been dropped. Sadly, even horrific as this may read, it is none the less true.

For thousands more of course, there would never again be the sight of home. They lay on the banks of the Kwai-noi and the Meklong, and along the route of the notorious railway which had caused their deaths. They covered the jungles of Siam and rested in a thousand lonely places between Rangoon and Bangkok. All that remained as evidence of our slavery was the rusting nails and tattered remnants of clothing cast aside when the days of slavery were over.

And as time went by that evidence bowed down before the power of nature, and only the mental image remained.

When, after a long period of hospitalisation, I sailed for home, I hoped I'd left behind all the things I'd grown to hate. I really thought the world was changing.

We had written to our people and been given every kind of hospitality by the authorities. Now we were to have a real feast, provided by volunteers still doing their bit for returning soldiers: a stew which tasted delightful, and to follow, something we'd dreamed of in the camps. Rice pudding, made with wholesome rice, and thick cream.

Alas, in an instant of uncontrollable fury, we stood up, and flung the plates into the air, to the consternation of the cooks, and the alarm of our nurses.

Discharged from hospital, it was suggested by the doctor that I might benefit from a spell of not too hard physical work so that my body would gradually regain its former strength. Eager to start on a musical career for which I'd trained before the war, I nevertheless agreed to try some other work for a few months. I attended a labour exchange and explained what kind of work I wanted. The clerk nodded understandingly. There were a few jobs on his book of a physical nature that might suit me.

After signing innumerable papers, he pushed over the counter a folder for me to read.

'Employment is available,' I read, '. . . with the L.N.E.R. at stations in various parts of the country. Labour is required immediately for work on the permanent way . . .'

I looked at the clerk for a few seconds. Then I tore up the folder, and started to laugh. When I walked away, he was still standing with an extremely hurt expression upon his face, poor man.

Associations of P.O.W.'s formed themselves into a Federation. They urged the government to seek compensation from the Japs and in the end we received fifteen pounds each, or about seven shillings and sixpence for every month spent in the camps of the Far East. A Motion was debated in the House of Commons in which it was sought to establish that never again must P.O.W.'s be open to treatment such as we had received. Incredibly, it was opposed by some M.P.s who felt that it was all part of the risk a soldier took when he was called up.

We were beginning to realise that very few who hadn't experienced that time had the slightest understanding or compassion for us. That was the hardest thing to bear.

When the Captains and the Kings depart and the sounds of war are dimmed it is far too easy to forget the very things we had sworn to remember. For many there is so much more to think about and to achieve. Then the years go by and bitter memories are softened. Writing this, I appreciate the ease with which human nature can turn aside all noble feelings and concentrate entirely on living.

Unfortunately, for a great many men this happy state is not so easy to achieve.

Many who felt that they'd escaped the very worst flung at them by the Japanese have since found that time, far from being a healer, has proved to be an enemy.

Physical and mental wounds apparently healed, have returned to give countless hours of extra misery, and in the end their former life has come back to haunt them.

Tom died a few years ago, after living for some time in a private world of his own, peopled by ghosts: a world I found impossible to enter so that I could help.

Jeremy was luckier. He is now a doctor and lives in Africa where he specialises in tropical medicine. He certainly received primary education second to none.

Others, like Tom, have died and continue to die each year despite the care given by doctors who differ only from those in the camps in that they are able to provide drugs and every modern aid to assist them.

How astounding it is to recall the camp doctors and the lives they saved without aid of proper medicine. And it is to a generation of such men that I owe my life.

My own doctor would feel genuinely self-conscious if I praised his skill too much. To him, medical science is part of a job and he is probably unused to praise. Yet I owe him so much.

A year or two ago, I had cardiac trouble. For the hundredth time I was back in hospital and some of my past medical history came to light. I found myself being treated as a V.I.P. and my recovery was greeted with as much delight as if I'd been a Head of State.

I asked, as I frequently have asked, if they could tell me why the body resists attempts to kill it. They couldn't.

In the end many survived according to their strength and their will, plus the tender care of doctors and nurses. If other organisations and groups had the same profound feeling for caring, the world would eventually become the kind of place we all dream of. But alas, man is still as selfish and as forgetful as ever, and we do not yet merit this ideal.

It is believed in many quarters that integrity and kindliness get one nowhere in the modern world. When I hear this said I'm immediately reminded of a small priest who had refused to leave Singapore on one of the last ships to get away from the port in 1942.

Later on, he was sent up north and received a great amount of abuse from the Japanese because of his calling.

Absolutely without fear, he inspired us all by his quiet manner. Never more so as on the day he stood in silent prayer and a Japanese N.C.O. saw him. He was at once attacked and beaten terribly with a thick block of wood. The small priest showed complete disregard of this assault. Presently, he turned towards the Jap and said in a very quiet but firm voice: 'Please go away – can't you see I'm talking to someone?'

The sun shines occasionally through my window, although not in the manner of that eternal summer of Siam. Perhaps this should be enough for me or any who survived.

For make no mistake about it, some of us are very much in love with life. In the end, isn't that exactly what we struggled for? Isn't this the desire on which we placed our hopes when we were prisoners?

And whatever else has proved false, this life we hold on to is still worth living no matter how hard some may still have to struggle. That's what it was all about.

Tom's first words when we docked at Liverpool were brief.
'Well, chum – we've made it!'
It would be dreadful if I doubted him now.

Bill Duncan

Finis.

The Circle

The Circus

THE CIRCLE

Leo Rawlings

The beginning is the end and the end is the beginning.

If I was asked to give the exact moment when I began to waver in my hatred for the Japanese I don't think I could do so.

Ever since the end of World War II and my release from a Japanese Prison Camp in Singapore, I along with thousands of other ex-P.O.W's, had hated the Japanese nation with a hatred that knew no bounds. The diabolical, murderous behaviour of our former captors had burnt an indelible scar across our minds, as well as our bodies. No way did we ever intend to forget it, no matter how long we lived! This was the general outlook and decision of practically all former Japanese prisoners.

During my incarceration in many camps and on the dreaded, notorious 'Railway of Death' I had recorded many incidents and events concerning the 1st Malayan Campaign, the Fall of Singapore and three and a half years as a P.O.W. These records were in the form of tiny sketches and scribbled notes on rough paper. Brushes I made from my own hair and paints from roots and clay. The illustrations and records had been called the most conclusive and accurate text book of that period of history by people all over the world, many of whom had also been P.O.W's.

Subsequently, but only after great difficulties and tribulations, I published a fully illustrated book on my experiences entitled 'And the Dawn came up like Thunder' containing most of the pictures I had produced in captivity. No British Publisher would entertain the book, calling it too horrific and quite unacceptable to the public, so I had no alternative but to produce the record of man's

163

inhumanity to man myself, believing that such events should be exposed and made known to the world in the hope that they would never be allowed to happen again.

Some 15,000 copies had eventually been sold all over the world, collecting many congratulations and thanks from people in all walks of life. 1972 was the year of publication and in 1978, getting on with my job as a freelance artist, I considered the matter closed once and for all. My moral debt to my fallen comrades had been paid in full.

Much was my surprise, therefore, when I received a letter from a friend of mine, Bill Duncan, in Scotland. Bill, also an ex-Jap P.O.W., had written an illuminating contribution to my book and was a man dedicated like myself to truth and the exposure of history in the cause of progress.

His letter both amazed and disgusted me for it spoke of his newly acquired friend, a Japanese gentleman who claimed to be deeply concerned with the plight of former P.O.W's and was the originator of a world peace movement called "The Bridge of Kindness". It appeared that the Japanese gentleman, Mr. Nagase Takashi, had read my book and wished to translate and publish it in Japan for the benefit of present and future generations. It was very evident that Bill fully supported Mr. Nagase and had written to me to try to persuade me to sell the Japanese rights to the Japanese.

Bill Duncan had hardly worked since the end of the war due to very severe health problems directly caused by his own terrible experiences as a P.O.W. He had been tortured excessively for long periods by the Kempi Tai, the dreaded Japanese Secret Police whose rule in the Far Eastern P.O.W. Camps was absolute.

I was horrified and disgusted that Bill, now a very sick man, should have allowed himself to be taken in by this Mr. Nagase Takashi who, it appeared, was himself a former interpreter for the Kempi Tai and had witnessed scenes of horror and inhumanity on a vast scale.

I at once refused to entertain the Japanese overtures of peace, believing it to be a 'face saver' only and an effort on the part of our former enemies to get round their foul crimes against P.O.W's.

Some weeks passed after my almost abusive reply to Bill Duncan in which I accused him of going pro-Jap and mentally senile with it ! Then another letter arrived from Duncan; this time he set down facts and figures about Mr. Nagase's war record which he had researched himself to great extent. Nagase, it appeared, had been completely cleared of all war crimes, even being supported and spoken for by several other P.O.W's at the War Crimes Courts. At no time had Nagase been guilty of ill treatment or cruelty in any way whatsoever. Furthermore, he had himself been threatened with execution by his superiors for protesting against Japanese behaviour to P.O.W's.

Since the war Nagase had been seriously ill himself and had finally recovered to begin a constant dedication to peace and revelation of war crimes committed by his own people.

For some time I considered this new evidence. Knowing Bill Duncan to be a man of principle and good intent I was still unconvinced and shelved the matter. I did not reply. Time passed again and one day I received a letter from Japan. Mr. Nagase himself had written to me stating his case in detail.

On reading his words a change came over me. I felt a strange motivation to go along with the idea that my book should perhaps be read by my former enemies. 'I may tell the bastards the truth, once and for all', I thought. And then the end would justify the means.

Many more letters now flowed between the Japanese gentleman and myself. Each one made me realise, grudgingly, that there was at least one Jap who thought as I did. The sincerity contained in his letters left no doubt in my mind that he was genuine in his aims and so, finally, in 1979, I allowed him to purchase the Japanese rights of my book for a nominal sum, more as a gesture than a commercial undertaking. I had little optimism of the final outcome and did not believe for one moment that the book would ever see daylight.

In September, 1979, I received a shock. Not only was the book now approaching final print but already causing a great sensation all over Japan, almost a guaranteed success! Furthermore, I was invited to go to Japan as guest of Nagase and attend a celebration party in my honour.

Slowly the full impact of what lay ahead of me sank in. Dare I go? Maybe it was a cheap stunt to exploit me and all ex-P.O.W's in order to gain national credit for my former enemies, and particularly Mr. Nagase himself?

'You must go', my family and close friends urged me. 'You owe it to the lads (P.O.W's) to go and give our side of the story in person. You can't let them down now.'

Of course I would go, I told myself, downing a pint of beer in my local pub one evening. An hour later, back home, watching the T.V. film 'Inside Japan' I faltered and hesitated. Mortally terrified of reliving the past all over again in a strange land on the far side of the world; probably falling victim to the various minor health troubles which still beset me as a result of the war years — neurosis, digestive troubles, indifferent eyesight, acute nervous tension etc — and out of reach of my devoted M.D here in Harpenden.

For days at a time I see-sawed in my mind. I often woke during the night in a sweat, terrified at the challenge awaiting me yet defiantly grasping at straws of confidence to take me on to another day of indecision.

More and more news from Japan arrived; endless publicity in the Japanese press acclaiming me and my book; hundreds of Japanese waiting to meet me — and so it went on.

I struggled to find an excuse, however small, to extricate me from the web I had allowed myself to be ensnared in. I couldn't afford to go, I told myself. Business was not good and I owed a good many bills. Agreed, my trip was paid for but I would lose heavily whatever happened.

Slowly the dreaded day drew near. Dreaded? It should have been joyous but it wasn't. I had never flown in a 'plane in my life! I was not afraid to die in an air crash — BUT! As in a nightmare of doubts and secret fears I eventually took control of myself. I claimed to believe in God, where was my faith now?

Then I knew it had to be. Whatever lay ahead had to be faced, whether I wanted it or not. I consulted reliable clairvoyants I had known for years. All were adamant — GO! It is all good. Fear nothing, it is the turning point of your life and career. Consoled but still inwardly shaking I drove to Heathrow with my wife who was a tower of strength and, bidding a brief farewell, went through the boarding alley towards the Boeing 747 which was to transport me to the ends of the earth.

From the moment I stepped aboard the giant skyliner I was a different man. The past fell from my shoulders like a worn out garment. It is not untrue or blasphemous for me to say quite clearly that I felt the hand of God upon me. Never before had such exhilaration lifted my inner self. I walked to my seat with my feet treading air. Confident and assured. Flying is the end and the beginning. The end of cowardice and the beginning of trust — or so it was for me. Looking around me I thought that if indeed this was an ill-fated 'plane then I could do worse than end my earthly life with those around me. The competent aircrew and lovely air stewardesses of Singapore Airlines warmed my heart and I couldn't wait for take off.

The flight to Singapore was an experience I shall never forget. Perhaps hardened flyers may mock at these expressed emotions of a hitherto non-flyer but to me it was really living. The drifting clouds below me seemed like a soothing veil of enchantment separating two worlds — fiction, which lay below, and beauty which was now my own special world.

As we approached Singapore I was favoured with a visit to the flight deck and watched the Island of my past — land of horror and despair — rise up on the distant horizon. Hovering as it seemed in space I looked down on God's world in spellbound wonder at the magnificent panorama of gold tipped cumulus and stratus clouds arranged like the entrance to Heaven itself.

A brief night in Singapore and then on to Osaka, Japan, the following morning in a D.C.10, again of Singapore Airlines, surrounded by lovely Asian girls who pampered me with excellent food and drinks. Approaching Osaka Airport the 'plane's descent caused me temporary pain in my right ear but on landing this was quickly forgotten by seeing the overwhelming efficiency of the Japanese officials who conveyed me through customs and arrival channels in record time. Everywhere I looked cleanliness surrounded me. Shining, polished floors reflected the masses of tired travellers hurrying to meet friends and relatives awaiting them at the airport reception area.

As in a dream I followed them and suddenly found myself the centre of flashing cameras. A small excited figure, instantly recognisable as Nagase Takashi, waved to me from the midst of a crowd and in seconds we were shaking hands like old friends. The fact that this man had been my hated enemy for almost forty years did not occur to me. We looked each other in the eye and I knew I was amongst friends.

A young Japanese reporter had come to interview me and he insisted on carrying my very weighty case. Hiroyasu Suda of one of Japan's top newspapers was slight of build but as he carried my case he assured me that this was his own small gesture of apology for my treatment as a P.O.W. His sincerity left no doubt in my mind that he meant it.

We proceeded to the nearby railway station to take the famous 'Bullet Train' to Kurashiki some 150 miles away. This luxurious epitome of rail travel needs to be seen to be believed. Scrupulously clean you could almost eat off the floors, it flashed with soundless speed on a track so smooth no vibration showed on the surface of my instantly supplied glass of iced water. It was brought by a smiling Japanese girl waitress who padded to our table in the restaurant car almost before we sat down.

Things were happening so fast I could hardly keep up with them. Already I was being plied with countless, yet courteously applied, queries from Mr. Suda on my travel experiences, my impressions of Japan and what I was feeling at that moment.

In no time at all, roughly one breathtaking hour, we were at Kurashiki where Magase's lovely wife Yosica awaited us with the car. Not allowed to handle my luggage or lift a finger, I found myself in the front seat next to Yosica who drove with skill and care to my hotel some distance away.

During the short journey I observed with amazement the clean, tidy, yet busy streets of the City. Everwhere the picture of control and order such as I had never seen before — certainly not in Britain since pre-war days.

Modest prosperity was evident on all sides though in no way opulent or vulgar.

Arriving at the Ivy Square Hotel, Kurashiki, I was entranced by the well constructed, beautiful building of fine red brick which had been built some five years earlier. It had an atmosphere of grace, good taste and, yet again I have to say it, efficiency unparalleled in any hotel I have ever been in — and I have seen many. My luggage was whisked away by two smiling young Japanese porters who bowed constantly to me like bobbing corks.

The vast foyer gleamed and shone with modulated though clear lighting as silent staff went about their work with cheerful competence. No small request or service was too much for them.

I was greeted by Mr. Asano, the Hotel Manager, warmly and with a kindly understanding smile of welcome. (Something many British Proprietors could do well to imitate!). Courtesy and good manners are just a very few of the assets which Japan can claim, and they come naturally without being overpatronizing.

The party to celebrate the acceptance of my book in Japan was set for Sunday, 30th May, and until that day I was escorted to various points of interest in the locality by students of Mr. Nagase's school of English. One of the places I visited was the sacred shrine of Shinto Warriors. A large, somewhat austere wooden building constructed in the traditional architecture of old Japan. Its beautiful roof of tiles curved gently in harmony with the surrounding terrain of low hills and trees.

Shinto ! The work suddenly rang a loud bell in my memory. Hadn't those warriors of this ancient order also partaken in the ravages of World War II ? Yet here was I about to meet the High Priest and attend the ceremony which, I had been told by Nagase, was to be held in my honour. Momentarily I hesitated, then realised that each year Nagase Takashi took a large party of ex Japanese soldiers back to Singapore and Tahiland to pay homage to Allied War dead. This year he had not been able to go because of illness so his wife, Yosica, had taken his place in their pilgrimage of humanity. In the face of such dedication to us P.O.W's I knew I could not insult them by declining to attend this solemn ceremony.

I took my place on the front wooden bench before the High Altar, a modest oblong of wood unadorned by bric-a-brac or ceremonial pomp and quite devoid of ostentation in any way. The High Priest, a tall, aged Japanese monk, shaven of head and clad only in white robes, came forward and, with his back to me, faced the shrine in silence. Suddenly behind me a great leather drum began to beat slowly but loudly. I lost count of the strokes, my head was singing. As the drum beat ceased a very strange feeling overcame me. A great peace settled on my mind and, without thinking, I got up and walking forward, knelt in silent prayer at the Altar. A prayer for all the dead who had fallen in past battles for Japan, the country they believed in for better or worse — just as we had done ourselves over centuries; not questioning our leadership but following blindly those who led us into battle. Could I fail to include ALL who had done their bit for their country? I could not.

My Japanese friends, for such I now felt they were, seemed a little amazed at my act of reverence to their cult but obviously silently pleased. I did not care. What I had done I had done for myself and all those I had fought with who were now in spirit. I felt they wished me to do so.

170

As a spiritualist I believe we are equal beyond the grave, whatever nationality.

The visit ended with my being conducted to the Priest's Council Chamber where I was given a tiny silver cup of rice wine and a small cake, similar to our own communion in principle and just as important to those in Japan as our form of worship is to us. I then signed the Visitors' Book, a rare honour I learned, with a long Japanese brush. I talked with the High Priest who had read my book and acknowledged its value to mankind. He spoke good English so I know his words were true. Leaving the shrine I was again conscious of a great peace upon me. It never left me during my whole stay in Japan and I still have it.

Sunday, March 30th dawned with a raging cold clogging my head, due, no doubt, to the change of temperature of Singapore's 99° to Japan's 58°. I felt like remaining in bed but too much had been planned for me to back out now.

At 11 a.m. I went downstairs to attend the party and a bevy of beautiful Japanese girls, adorned in gorgeous kimonos of varied colours met my eyes. Three huge round tables laden with food and drink were spaced at intervals in a vast room of the hotel. Throngs of quiet, smiling people watched me as I was led by the hand by Mrs. Nagase to a corner where two microphones set before a huge gold and pink coloured screen awaited me. Silently the throng of people assembled in a semi-circle and I gave a short speech of thanks for the welcome extended to me, including remarks concerning the futility of war and the consequences both nations had suffered as a result of past conflicts. All told about eight speeches were made by various people. Nagase Takashi himself, the president of the Hiroshima Shrine who was a school boy when the bomb fell and who, as a result, has no ears, only tiny mishapen stumps of flesh and half grown hands, and other people who had all read my book and agreed entirely with its contents.

As I listened through my Interpreter who stood at my elbow translating each phrase, I became aware that there in Japan the sufferings of my P.O.W. comrades was very

171

deeply felt and understood every bit as much as the plight of the Japanese survivors of the A bomb who continue to die horribly each year as a result of this monstrous act.

Tears ran down many faces as both these events of history were recounted and I knew beyond doubt at that moment that my visit to Japan had not been in vain.

Japan today is indeed fully conscious of its past history and not only aware but determined it must not happen again. They bear no hatred for those who dropped the bomb. They sorrow deeply for us, their victims, the P.O.W.'s, and indeed all who were tainted and warped, maimed and mutilated in action. They only ask this — that we remember but hate no more.

From the genuine love and friendship which was shown to all ex-P.O.W's through me on my Japanese visit I know Japan today is a fine country, worthy of a top place in the society of nations and worthy also of true forgiveness and honour. If they have forged ahead beyond other nations through enterprise and hard work they deserve every bit of it. I know, for I have been and seen for myself.

Before leaving I paid a visit to the Hiroshima Shrine in that now fine city, where thousands go each day to pay respects. I went round the large exhibition of horrors beyond the envisagement of the western mind. Thousands of women and children not only died in the holocaust but died in unspeakable agony, skinned from head to foot, their skin hanging from limbs like tissue paper. Hiroshima the City has been rebuilt. The Japanese people of that area of disaster have picked themselves up but they will bear their scars for many years to come. If we of the west truly believe in Jesus Christ or any other cult or denomination we cannot face our future on this earth unless we wholeheartedly work increasingly for peace, through remembrance.

Flying back to London again, surrounded with the luxury of modern day flying, relaxed now and full of a sense of relief that my ordeal was at last over, my thoughts went back to 1942 when first I had met the Japanese. Had I but dreamed for a moment what was ahead of me who knows what I would have done. That was the beginning of the circle, the circle which was to end with me feeling deep regard and even love for the descendents of those wielding the whip of conquest over me. During the dark days which followed the fall of Singapore I had slowly become aware of my spiritual senses — convinced also that no matter what my body was to endure, within me was a power which would bring me through. All people have this power, so very few accept it let alone try to use it. Deep Spiritual convictions grow in me as time passed and even in the darkest days I felt somehow that there was a reason for it all, a plan to be lived through and something of use to be done with my life.

Looking through the 'plane's window it all came clear to me. Through a former enemy who, had I but known it at the time was a friend in disguise, was as confused as I was, I had been allowed to establish a link which now, after almost forty years, would never be broken. A link of mutual understanding of many things. A bone of humanity which may, God willing, echo into the distant future to those yet to be born and give perhaps a little encouragement and heart when all seems finished. Nagase Takashi and his wife have performed a vital service to humanity in my opinion. Their courage and perseverance to promote understanding and kindness cannot go unnoticed. That they speak for very many other Japanese is without question in my mind evident. The treatment I received in Japan was far more than just to a former P.O.W. — it was to all the British people. Of this I am certain.

Throughout it all my Japanese adventure had taught me much. From having to master my fears of yesterday, my bitter, unceasing hatred which had almost ruined my health for so many years, I had taken a step forward that I would never regret. Gone was the hatred, gone was the illusion that the Japanese would never change. They had! Was this not the real Japan which, for a brief moment in history 1941-45 had taken a momentary step backward and paid dearly for it? It is a good country populated by good, living people. May it always be so. From what I have seen and experienced

I have every reason to believe that this will be the case.

Hatred is blind and to those who still doubt, to those who have not retraced their steps as I have done I would say: 'Cease your hatred now before it consumes you and lights the spark to a repetition of history. Accept the new generation of Japan as a vital contribution to today's world, our own future, our children's future and that of every nation. We depend upon it.'

On Reflection

ON REFLECTION

LEO RAWLINGS

The reaction of the Japanese people and press to my article "The Circle", published in the Asahi Evening News on 4th and 5th September 1980, has been most gratifying to me personally. It has also triggered off a great deal of comment from English people who have seen it, though in truth not all have agreed with my viewpoint.

This is quite understandable as I see it for until I came to Japan and saw for myself, I too was a sceptic of Japan's new approach to the past and future of world affairs.

There have been quite a number, however, who openly praise my words and agree entirely that the past must be forgiving if not completely forgotten in order that new generations may have at least a reasonable chance of reaching understanding with each other.

It is quite clear that there must be many men and women in both Japan and other countries who care but very little what happens to themselves or anyone else, for that matter. Due either to illness or unawareness of the world around them. One can scarcely expect a well balanced, objective view from someone suffering from radiation sickness or some other complaint attributable to war. Hundreds, possibly thousands of Japanese soldiers and civilians, literally waiting for their weary, pain ridden lives to end, can truthfully not be blamed for adopting a scathing, cynical attitude towards those of us who have been spared and allowed to profit, if only psychologically from our bitter past.

We must take these factors into account when trying to assess a Nation's reaction to the harrowing, and too often calamitous events happening around us, in almost every country in the world.

Perhaps I have been one of this world's most fortunate

mortals, in as much that I have made a journey through the valley of the shadow of death, and by the Grace of God, allowed to emerge into pastures of liberty and understanding of my fellow men. Not that I wish to dramatically make light of the journey, or of my final steps through the last grim portal of dread. It was pretty much hell all the way, for after the end of my captivity the road back to normal civilian life was fraught with upheavals and shocks, to say the very least of it.

For several years I now realise, I must have been a very difficult person to live with. What had been passed off as battle and stress fatigue during my incarceration period, was not even understood, let alone tolerated by my relatives and post war friends. Who could blame them? My comrades and I from the Eastern Prison Camps came to be regarded as neo-lunatics of very undesirable behaviour indeed.

During the last week of confinement in Changi Jail Camp, 1945, having been made to dig our own graves, my friend Eric Newman from Blackpool, and I made a solemn vow. Namely that if by a miracle we survived death, and returned home to England, we would be drunk for a whole year and have as many women as we could lay hands on.

It is true to say that we honoured our vow to the full. Well, at least I did!

It is not exactly something I am now proud of but neither am I ashamed of my confession, for the previous three and a half years had built up a wall of confusion in our minds which seemed to only go away for a brief spell when under alcoholic influence, or locked in the arms of a new lover. Our return to civilian life had been far too quick for sanity to establish itself decisively. From living as near naked skeletons in a festering graveyard of dead and dying men we were suddenly transported to our homes in a mere matter of weeks. To a world most of us never expected to see again if truth were told.

For many years to come our minds were to live and relive again and again the frightfulness of the hell camps along the River Kwai and down to Singapore's Changi Jail. There we had little outlet or opportunity to express our desires, even if we entertained any beyond freedom and food. Sex rarely ever entered our minds as a diet of 90% rice does nothing for one's genitals. You can take my word for it!

It is therefore I think fair to say that we needed our booze and women. We probably enjoyed the booze more than the women if we were honest for we (me especially) were out of practice with affairs of the heart and girls probably found us anything but God's gift to women.

Reviewing those distant years now througn older and more sober eyes I realise the simple facts, which though plain before us then we could see nothing but the waving flag and the imagined glory of suffering and destroying fellow humans. The truth was that the means of our liberty had been bought at an appalling price by the people of Hiroshima and Nagasaki. Had we even realised the full effects of this act I doubt if it would have cost us any sleep. Chance is we would have wished it on the whole Japanese Nation.

What the Japanese were thinking at that time is not possible for me to imagine but in all probability feelings were of a similar tempo. The whole world had gone mad and sanity was still an infant.

To us released ex P.O.W.s it was justice that these frightful bombs had been used to bring the six year war to an end, and destroying our hated enemies. Doubtless to the Japanese it was the foulest of injustice that innocent women and children should suffer and expire in that inhuman manner. A viewpoint I entirely agree with now. Only all these years after the event can either of us see, or try to see it in perspective.

Justice and injustice are man-made words, designed to set a standard of behaviour and control of emotions. In times of war these rules would seem not to apply.

Hatreds die hard for we are apt to remember only the evil that mankind commits against his fellow humans, and forget the good deeds. I believe it takes great courage to cease hating. It also needs an awareness of the outlook and age old customs of those we hate by tradition or popular decree, and these factors are not easy to arrive at.

Quite often, even when they are discovered, one's motives are suspect and cause only more distrust than existed before. So the process of understanding calls for humility at all times. I ask pardon of my readers if my opinions appear too sweeping and generalising. They are not intended to be like this, and I voice only my own personal feelings and views that life has encouraged me to nurture. It is still amazing to me that I find myself analysing my past life in respect to the Japanese people, who for so many years I hated and despised without remorse or regret. I can only say how very happy it makes me to have been helped to break through the barrier of time and ignorance which had become my daily outlook, by you the people of Japan, and Nagase Takashi in particular. This is to me real justice for I believe we have helped each other along the highway of truth and humility for the sake of those who will follow.

When in the beautiful Ivy Square Hotel, Kurashiki, under the charming and capable management of Mr. Asano, I would think to myself on occasions that on that very ground, though not in that Hotel for it had not then been built, Japanese soldiers and servicemen had in all certainty relaxed on leave from the conflict behind them in the Far East, or awaited their call to a foreign field to fight and probably die as my comrades were doing also.

Watching the exotic Carp in the Hotel pools I imagined myself as a Japanese Officer or Trooper spending his last hours of liberty in a garden with his girlfriend or wife and children; walking meditatively along the canal which runs through the old city and counting the hours until his departure to war, stoically hiding his emotions and determined to honour his country and Emperor to the fullest extent. It was easy for me to do this as I only needed to recall my own embarkation leave in 1941, prelude to entraining to Liverpool and the awaiting troopship, to put myself in the place of my former enemy on leave. How excited and confident we had been then, my comrades and I. Full of self induced courage, mainly out of a beer mug, and totally unaware of what destiny would now demand of us.

So it must have been in that lovely old Japanese city. Even with the more emotionally controlled oriental. No doubt tears were not easily hidden or held back as final sayonaras were made and solemn eyed troops bowed low before marching away to a bloody battle zone which was to claim them in countless thousands, or eventually allow their mangled shattered bodies to return to be honoured and preserved like museum pieces.

Haven't we seen it all before? There are still those in this foolish world who revel, as we did, in war and its false glamour, bent only on greed, conquest and power.

Their lesson has yet to be learned. It can only be realised through pain, misery and humility.

Japan is now, as I see it, well on the road to becoming a super power. Having had the maximum experience in war and peace she is influencing and leading many other world peoples in advanced methods of science and technology, and her impact on tomorrow's world can be nothing but good. Her dedicated soldiers, sailors, airmen and citizens of the past all contributed to make that possible. But above all the Japanese people as a whole must take pride of place for showing amazing fortitude and forbearance in surviving the horror of the first atomic blasts. It is my sincere and indeed, desperate hope that those Nations possessing nuclear weapons will think long and carefully about the possible outcome to their own carelessness and political see-saws, before plunging humanity yet again into the cauldron of fire.

Next time the phoenix may not survive the heat.

The
Damnation
of
Earth

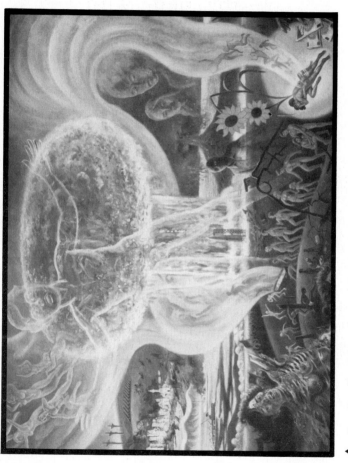

▲ *Leo Rawlings thought-provoking painting The Damnation of Earth*

End of the world
by the man who
has been to hell

Leo Rawlings established himself as an artist with a unique record of that appalling theatre of conflict. Today, at 65, he still suffers from the nervous after-effects. He lives in Berkhamsted in quiet peace. But his last important painting about the war is anything but peaceful.

It is a huge canvas called the Damnation of Earth and tells of Leo Rawlings' feelings on war, the atomic age, the nuclear threat and the world we live in. Mr. Rawlings believes it is an important comment of today's most important international debate.

His apocalyptic painting of the Damnation of Earth is his latest major work of art to derive from his own dreadful sufferings in the Far East during the early 1940's. A letter he received from the only survivor of 200 children caught in their schoolyard by the blast of Hiroshima persuaded him, in 1979 to allow his book to be translated. That decision also released much of his hidden, deep long-suffering hate.

Mr. Rawlings visited the man who wrote to him and later arranged the translation and publication of his book.

He was Akhiro Takahashi. His occupation now is curator of the peace memorial in Hiroshima. Like most Japanese, he has set himself to achieve peace.

The visit to Japan, provided Mr. Rawlings with the inspiration to complete his Damnation of Earth. "It shows all of life and slow death. It shows childhood through the stages of life to terrorism and conflict and death.

"It has the Middle East conflict and symbol of youth looking and wondering what it all is. It holds all the horrors of war and the bombs."

The picture also includes the Japanese schoolchildren running from the blast with their bodies burning. "They have learned from their experience as no other country has."

Lord Mountbatten of Burma AF
Launches book at the
Wig & Pen Club, Strand, London
OCTOBER 29th 1972

I was in